THE PRODIGAL SON

Wayne Hazen

TEACH Services, Inc.
PUBLISHING
www.TEACHServices.com • (800) 367-1844

World rights reserved. This book or any portion thereof may not be copied or reproduced in any form or manner whatever, except as provided by law, without the written permission of the publisher, except by a reviewer who may quote brief passages in a review.

The author assumes full responsibility for the accuracy of all facts and quotations as cited in this book. The opinions expressed in this book are the author's personal views and interpretations, and do not necessarily reflect those of the publisher.

This book is provided with the understanding that the publisher is not engaged in giving spiritual, legal, medical, or other professional advice. If authoritative advice is needed, the reader should seek the counsel of a competent professional.

Copyright © 2025 Wayne Hazen
Copyright © 2025 TEACH Services, Inc.
Published in Calhoun, Georgia, USA
ISBN-13: 978-1-4796-1828-6 (Paperback)
ISBN-13: 978-1-4796-1829-3 (ePub)
Library of Congress Control Number: 2025901885

All Scripture quotations, unless otherwise indicated, are taken from the King James Version of the Bible. Public Domain.

Scripture quotations marked NIV are taken from the *Holy Bible, New International Version*®. Copyright © 1973, 1978, 1984, International Bible Society. Used by permission.

Illustrations by Wayne Hazen

Published by

DEDICATION

This book is dedicated to Velma Doris Picknell Hazen,
whose faith, compassion, and gentle influence so profoundly colored
the canvas of her son's spirit.

May you rest in peace, mother, until we reunite before Jesus.

Special thanks to Dee and Ernie Scott
for sponsoring the publication of this book.

Table of Contents

Introduction 9

Prologue: Treacherous Waters 11

Chapter 1: A Fresh Canvas 15

Chapter 2: Sketching Bobbie 18

Chapter 3: Misadventures with Phillip 22

Chapter 4: A Fellow Prodigal and a Friendly Seeker 27

Chapter 5: Sobering Surrealness 32

Chapter 6: Mrs. Romano's Daughter 35

Chapter 7: A Portrait of Hatred 40

Chapter 8: Running a Gauntlet 43

Chapter 9: The Joy and Peril of Good Painting 46

Chapter 10: Nightlife 48

Chapter 11: Traffic and Accidents 54

Chapter 12: Sketching Bobbie Again 62

Chapter 13: Pastoral Scene 65

Chapter 14: A Warning and Grace 69

Chapter 15: Surprising Encounters 74

Chapter 16: Fishing of a Sort 81

Chapter 17: Impressions of Junior Year 84

Chapter 18: Beware the Tides 87

Chapter 19: Peer Critique 91

Chapter 20: Monique Returns 94

Chapter 21: An Evening with Connie 97

Chapter 22: Broken Figures 100

Chapter 23: A Civil Consultation and a Jarring Awakening 110

Chapter 24: The Fruits of One's Labor 116

Chapter 25: The Samaritan and the Artist 118

Chapter 26: Surely He Will Save You 125

Chapter 27: New Poses 131

Chapter 28: Warrior Medics 134

Chapter 29: A Stilled Life 136

Chapter 30: Among the Living 139

Chapter 31: A High Price 142

Chapter 32: The Old Has Gone 145

Chapter 33: I Prepare a Place for You 149

Table of Contents

Chapter 34: The Greatest Artist 153

Chapter 35: Illuminating Grace 158

Chapter 36: On Solid Ground 162

Epilogue: At Home 167

Bibliography 169

The LORD is my shepherd; I shall not want.

He maketh me to lie down in green pastures: he leadeth me beside the still waters.

He restoreth my soul: he leadeth me in the paths of righteousness for his name's sake.

Yea, though I walk through the valley of the shadow of death, I will fear no evil: for thou art with me; thy rod and thy staff they comfort me.

Thou preparest a table before me in the presence of mine enemies: thou anointest my head with oil; my cup runneth over.

Surely goodness and mercy shall follow me all the days of my life: and I will dwell in the house of the LORD for ever.

– Psalm 23

So do not fear, for I am with you; do not be dismayed, for I am your God. I will strengthen you and help you; I will uphold you with my righteous right hand.

– Isaiah 41:10 (NIV)

Introduction

This book is a journey into the life of a modern-day prodigal son whom we will call Eric.

Raised in the embrace of ultra-conservative Seventh-day Adventists, he grappled with the need to break free from his parents' constraints; the rigid rules dictating his actions on Saturdays and the limitations on his choice of friends. As he matured, these restrictions became increasingly burdensome, and he yearned for his independence.

The Lord had given Eric talent in the fine arts, and he dreamed of becoming a great artist. He felt an inner-city art school would be the best place to realize his dream. He ventured out of his rural home at eighteen. The city's allure, freedom from rigid rules, and a chance to test his mettle against the real world beckoned him.

Unbeknownst to Eric, the biblical principles of the Psalms, instilled in him by his mother, had deeply influenced his values. She had shaped the direction of his life, even during times when his thinking and actions pushed the boundaries. When he left home, her words echoed in his ears: "You're a diamond in the rough, and God will polish off the rough edges."

This book shares Eric's experiences, both good and bad, over a three-and-one-half-year period in art school. You will see God's grace and the Holy Spirit working in young adults who were taught from early childhood the principles of eternal value from the Bible.

Ellen White refers to "the grace of self-forgetfulness" (Mind, Character, and Personality, 275.4) which "imparts to the life such an unconscious grace" (Education, 237). Even if they go astray like Eric did, God never forgets His children! Not only that, He is able to use people's character, shaped by those Bible teachings throughout childhood, for His purposes.

As you read, it is the prayer of the author that your faith would be strengthened.

PROLOGUE

Treacherous Waters

The wind had strengthened. Eric was hiking out on a close reach, and the sailboat was skipping along at speed. As the boat hit the crest of a small wave, the spray came inboard from the bow, drenching him from head to toe. A heavy jacket protected him somewhat, but it was October and quite cold.

Eric's passion for sailing was second only to his passion for art! He was so excited about the ease of handling the boat and the whole sailing experience that he forgot the cardinal rule: to keep his eyes on the water around him, and on the sky as well. As soon as he passed out of the harbor beyond the lee of the breakwater, the wind hit with such unexpected force that Eric lost control of the main sheet, causing the boat to heel all the way over on its beam, which laid the mast and mainsail out in the water.

This normally would not have become a life-threatening situation, but several things came together to put Eric's life in danger. The gale force wind was pushing against the bottom of the boat, forcing him farther from the land. Eric was getting heavy wave motion with a receding tide. And Eric had forgotten to tie a knot in the main sheet, which had gone all the way through the blocks and was lying out in the water alongside the mast and sail.

Eric jumped out on the centerboard, holding on for dear life as the boat started filling with water. He knew that he could not pull it upright unless the wind stopped. The boat had good flotation devices, but it would soon be too full to sail.

He figured he was about a mile from shore. He would more than likely die of exposure in a very short length of time. His fingers had already reached the point of numbness. Between the water temperature in the 50s and the wind chill, he would not have a chance to survive.

He knew he had lost control and was at the mercy of a very angry sea! He started praying for his life as he held onto the shrouds. "Lord, this is it. Your will be done." He closed his eyes and started repeating this prayer. He felt himself letting go.

"I cried with my whole heart; hear me, O LORD: I will keep thy statutes. I cried unto thee, save me, and I shall keep thy testimonies" (Ps. 119:145-146, KJV).

At that moment, the wind died almost completely. With his weight on the centerboard, the boat righted itself. Eric was able to pull himself back into the boat. He lay on the little deck, exhausted, thanking Jesus for his life.

He was still in great danger, so his adrenaline kicked in. As the boom swung inward, he grabbed the main sheet and thrust it back through the blocks as quickly as he could, then through the jam cleat. He tied a knot in the end of the sheet, grabbed the tiller arm, and pulled the sheet in tight enough to go on a starboard tack. He then went close hauled and started back into the harbor. The waves were now small and choppy. He changed his course to a beam reach. Finally, after getting in the lee of the breakwater, he was out of danger. God had just saved his life! He was sure of that. Eric would always remember this.

His friend Johnny was waiting on the beach to pick him up with the boat trailer. Eric did not say much as they drove back to Johnny's apartment. Johnny had earlier expressed his concern about Eric sailing on such a cold and windy day. This type of sailing, known as "frostbiting," was usually only done by experienced sailors. Eric had plenty of experience on big lakes; however, he lacked knowledge of the ocean, especially the tides which created the currents. Eric knew that Johnny was more experienced on the ocean, but he had been insistent upon sailing, so Johnny did not try to talk him out of it. That decision had almost cost Eric his life!

Eric finally spoke. "I guess I was pretty headstrong, wasn't I? But for God's saving grace, and prayer, I would not be alive. You know, Johnny, I just wasn't listening to my conscience. You are a good ocean sailor. You did not go with me because it was not worth it to put your life in danger. I should have gotten the hint. In the future, I hope I can learn to be wiser."

They parked and walked up the steps to Johnny's second-floor apartment. Johnny opened the door. Eric could finally get warm.

CHAPTER 1

A Fresh Canvas

Eric's first days at art school were scary. He realized that everyone had his skill level or better at drawing. He soon felt great, however, knowing that all these people were just like him. Being in class with forty other fine art students was an amazing experience! There were printmakers, painters, graphic designers, and sculptors. Eric felt that he had arrived … he was finally happy and at peace with the world.

After three months living with a family outside of town and making a tedious commute, Eric decided to stay in the city. He settled on an old Victorian hotel that was two blocks long and three blocks away from the school, which had been a grand hotel in the days of the clipper ships. Eric had two roommates at first. One was a prizefighter named David, who was always jumping rope and hitting a punching bag. His other roommate, Phillip, was a fellow art student. He was always smoking and staying up quite late reading novels. It was hard for Eric to find quiet time to sleep and to breathe fresh air!

The old hotel where Eric lived was a place that not only housed poor art students but also gay people, prostitutes, and very poor people, many of whom were alcoholics. The owner, Mr. Jones, was a very kind man who was slowly renovating the hotel, and he allowed these people to pay only $10 per week for a room.

The other end of the two-block hotel had fallen into disrepair and was tumbling down. It had broken-down doors and rooms without roofs; but this was a great place for the homeless of the city to hang out in. In the winter, the hotel was lifesaving for those who would have frozen living on the street.

The hotel became the epicenter of Eric's world, along with the road that ran in front of the hotel, Third Street. He walked to school in the morning and back in the evening along that street. He stopped at a sandwich shop for dinner most evenings on his way home. Junior, the building manager, had recommended it to him. It was called Romano's and was run by Marisa Romano and her daughter, Monique. Mrs. Romano was used to the art students. A kind, gentle person, she would cheerfully bring food to the tables and talk briefly with each of her customers.

After his evening meal, Eric usually went back to the art school or to his hotel to paint or draw until late in the evening. He soon learned that when it got dark, prostitution and drug activity in the area increased. Sellers and buyers moved quickly through the crowd … almost imperceptibly, unless you were streetwise.

CHAPTER 2

Sketching Bobbie

Many times, as Eric and Phillip were walking toward the hotel after school, an old streetwalker named Bobbie (she was likely in her forties) would call down to them from a second-floor window across the street. She would say, "Hey, sonny, come on up. I can give you the best time of your life."

In the window next to her was Bobbie's roommate, a Hispanic woman named Luce. Her lips covered half of her face because of the way she painted on her lipstick. She was different from Bobbie, in that she was very quiet and showed just enough of her "wares" to draw older men to converse with her.

When Bobbie called out, Phillip would make an obscene gesture or a face to Bobbie. Other art students would walk by and yell at the older inhabitants of the second floor with insults and harsh words. They were very crude, and Eric did not identify with them at all! He would say, "You're very beautiful, but no thanks," and keep walking.

Eventually, Bobbie began to swear at Phillip and Eric. She would ask, "Sonny, are you gay?" Then she would say, "I bet you can't ..." with a string of expletives. Finally, she would give them the finger and turn around.

Through all Bobbie's banter, Eric kept an even disposition, and if she caught his eye, he just smiled at her. At first this made her quite angry, but as days and months went by and he continued with the kind expression, she would just look at him. Meanwhile, Eric became quite captivated by Bobbie. Sometimes, in the latter part of the evening when she was at her most animated and expressive, he disappeared into the shadows with his sketchpad to draw her.

One evening, when Eric was walking home after dark with his sketchpad under his arm and his pencil box sticking out of his jacket, he heard a voice say, "Stop, I want to talk to you."

Eric turned around but did not see anybody. He continued to walk toward his hotel, then he heard the voice again: "Please stop." Eric half-turned, looked up, and realized Bobbie was the one speaking. Months before, he would have been afraid, but now he was not. He started walking across the street toward Bobbie's building.

She said, "Stay over there where I can see you. What's your name, Sonny?"

> Months before, he would have been afraid. He started walking across the street toward Bobbie's building.

"I'm Eric. You're Bobbie, right? How can I help you?"

"I have just one question for you, Eric. What makes you so different? In my world, people only appear to be nice if they get something, but you don't treat any of us badly."

Eric's answer was simple: "I believe we are all God's children. It is only right that we respect one another. I consider you one of God's beautiful, created beings. No matter who you are or what you do, you are His, and He loves you."

When he finished, Bobbie turned abruptly and walked away from the upper window, disappearing into the blackness. Eric continued to stand there for a moment, and then he resumed walking toward the hotel.

His thoughts were mixed up, and questions began to arise in his mind. Where had she come from? He wanted to find out more about her. At least now, he felt, he had broken through her rough exterior. Bobbie was allowing him into the private world of her mind, little by little. Eric decided that his prayers for her had made the difference.

CHAPTER 3

Misadventures with Phillip

At times Eric's friendship with Phillip was quite annoying; at other times, it was a load of laughs and just plain fun.

Phillip had grown up in the city. He had no real purpose in life other than just having a fun time being an artist. His dad and mom were very wealthy and absent from home most of the time, so they were happy to have him go to art school, which kept him off the street. In time, they rented him a gallery space where he could try to sell his paintings. Phillip tried very hard but simply lacked talent. On occasion, however, he did sell paintings.

Phillip once observed that Eric was not street-smart. He said he was older and wiser and could be a big help to Eric, the country boy. However, Phillip was always getting into trouble because he was trying to be part of the "in crowd." On several occasions he was punched in the face and his nose was broken.

In truth, the first time was not his fault. It happened when he and Eric were walking toward the docks to do "plain air" painting. It was early spring, and the streets were usually covered in ice and snow. The ice had melted this day and made holes in the surface of the street. As cars went by, they would splash water onto the pedestrians on the sidewalk. Phillip and Eric were soaked.

They passed a Mercedes Benz parked by an apartment building when a group of teenagers ran up from behind them. One of the teens reached out and ripped the hood ornament off of the Mercedes, then they kept running down the street. Suddenly, the owner of the car appeared and yelled at Phillip! Before he could say a word, the man hit him in the face with his fist. Phillip went crashing down to his knees with blood spurting from his nose, turning the snow on the ground red. The owner of the Mercedes ran off, still yelling angrily at Phillip.

Phillip's nose was big to start with and was now squashed to one side, almost completely flat. Eric tried to lift him to his feet but could not. After another five or ten minutes, Phillip rose and Eric was able to help him stumble back to the hotel. As they entered the lobby, Junior came out from behind his desk, immediately taking charge and assessing the situation.

Junior had come to the neighborhood about five years ago and started working for Mr. Jones as the building manager. He was also a

Vietnam veteran who had medic training. He ushered them into a back room and led Phillip to an upright chair without saying a word. Junior placed both hands on Phillip's face and twisted his nose back into place with crunching sounds. Phillip howled in pain, tears running down his face. Then Junior asked Eric what had happened while he brought ice from the refrigerator and put a pack on Phillip's nose.

Junior said that he should stay there for an hour or so and then ought to get the injury better-dressed. Later that afternoon, Eric helped Phillip onto the bus and talked briefly to the good-natured bus driver. He gave directions to his roommate's house (Phillip was still pretty distracted by the pain). Phillip's parents could help him get his nose taken care of.

Phillip's nose was broken for the second time when he tried to use a fake ID to get into an exclusive club. Eric and Junior came to his aid again that time. Phillip could not stay out of trouble and always dragged Eric into it! Eventually, as a result, while Eric still liked Phillip, he decided to move to a smaller studio in the hotel and room by himself. They became better friends once they were no longer rooming together.

On one occasion, Phillip invited Eric and several other art students to his new apartment (after Eric left, his former roommates also relocated) to draw a nude model. Phillip always put a lot of money into his parties, and he would usually provide catering. This was no exception! There were sandwiches of several kinds, pizzas, hors d'oeuvres, and some special sweet cakes that contained strawberries mixed with some sort of pudding or yogurt. Eric had a cheese pizza and a couple of small sandwiches.

Then Eric and four other students were ushered into the living room, where the model, Joanne, was sitting wearing a gown. There were only two easels, so Eric elected to sit on the floor with his pad and draw her from below. This would give a more dynamic perspective.

Joanne was one of the newer models from the art school. She had only been working there for a few weeks. Everyone knew that Phillip had tried to date her, but she always seemed to have an excuse not to. In class she would walk around to look at the work. On the last two occasions, she had spent time talking to Eric. She talked to many students, so Eric didn't think anything of it. She seemed quite nice, even if she did have a bit of a risqué reputation. Any bit of communication between the two of them went well.

She was a good model. The evening wore on, and eventually he and Phillip were the only ones left drawing. After it had gotten very late, Phillip suggested that Eric could stay and sleep on the couch. Phillip's apartment had two small bedrooms; Joanne was going to sleep in one of them, and Phillip, of course, was going to sleep in the other. Eric was very tired, so he agreed to stay if Phillip could spare an extra blanket. Phillip brought out an old sleeping bag and a blanket, and at 1:30 a.m., Eric fell asleep.

Sometime during the early morning hours, Eric awoke to a voice calling his name. In the half-light from the streetlight outside, he made out a dim figure beckoning him. Suddenly, he was wide awake. He said, "Is that you, Joanne?"

"Yes, it's me," she said. "I'm freezing cold. Would you mind if I snuggled up to you to keep warm? But please come to where I am sleeping because we cannot fit on the couch."

> *Eric finally caught his breath. "Please, Joanne, I would like to get to know you better, but not like this."*

All his red flags went up! It might have been a legitimate request, since the heat had been off for some time, but he still felt a little bit trapped. "OK, just until you get warmed up," he said.

Eric was still dressed except for his shoes. When he entered the bedroom, she had a small nightlight on and was already under the covers. She said, "Please hurry." To his shock and surprise, when she rolled back the covers for him to climb in, she was completely naked!

Eric caught his breath. He had not realized how beautiful she was up close. For a moment he was unsure of what to do. In a state of shock, he did not say anything.

Joanne lay there in a very suggestive pose. She reached out her hand and quietly said, "I need you tonight, Eric. Come get close to me and warm me up. No strings attached ... just two boats passing on the sea in the night. We can just be friends tomorrow, as usual."

Eric finally caught his breath. "Please, Joanne, you are a fine and beautiful woman, but I cannot take advantage of you this way. I would like to get to know you better, but not like this."

"Don't you like me, Eric?" she asked.

"Yes, of course, I do," he said, "but I won't violate you."

Suddenly, Joanne sat up and covered herself with the blankets. She said, "Do you know something? You are the first man who has rejected my invitation! I am not sure how to take it. Am I that unattractive? If you don't hate me and will still be my friend, I will try to forget my mistake."

Eric smiled at her uneasily. "As long as we can develop a friend relationship, I'll continue to get to know you."

Joanne smiled. "I would like that very much."

Eric looked at her for a moment. Then he said, "I guess you'll be warm enough." He walked out of the room and closed the door. While lying on the couch, his mind jumped from one topic to another. Eric gave up on sleeping for the rest of the night.

CHAPTER 4

A Fellow Prodigal and a Friendly Seeker

Eric's other original roommate, David, had left a very restrictive religious home as well. Because David came from just outside the city, his parents were close enough to have continual contact with him. His parents were evangelical and tried to get him to fit their mold.

Eric had begun to realize that those types of parents, though well-meaning, were driving their children away. Children, himself included, needed to see the loving nature of Jesus in the discipline that parents gave. Kids needed to know that their parents truly loved them; that it was not just an ego trip and a power struggle. Many young people, Eric saw, were more like the prodigal son than the son who stayed home and did everything "right."

When David was sixteen or seventeen, and apparently on his own, he had chosen to take up boxing as a career. He put on the gloves and started going to the gym. He was too heavy to be a lightweight, so he became a middleweight. While they all lived together, Phillip and Eric tried to support him as best they could by being in his corner at each match. Most of the men at the fights were large bodybuilder types. Eric even recognized one as the bouncer who had broken Phillip's nose at the exclusive club.

It was possible that David had the skill and the ability to do all the moves of a good fighter. His big weakness was that if he sustained a hit to the face, he went down for the count. At his second fight, for instance, David lasted a minute and a half. He was hit on the right cheek just under his eye and went down. He had a black eye for two weeks. After losing four fights badly in the first round, David decided to give up boxing and started studying to become a chef.

After Eric moved out of Phillip's apartment, he never saw David again. He had hoped to get to know him better. When David was not focused on boxing, they had had some good conversations about why they were both still in love with Jesus (but not their respective churches).

Soon Eric developed a good friendship with another art student named Johnny. They would compete in the classes that they took together. Johnny did not smoke or drink and seemed interested in a cleaner lifestyle than most. Another reason Eric took a liking to Johnny was that, having grown up by the ocean, Johnny had built several small sailboats. Eric had learned to sail when he was very young.

On the downside, Johnny was always questioning Eric about his church. He would ask, "What church do you belong to?"

Eric would always reply, "Why do you want to know?"

One day, he finally got tired of the questioning. He told Johnny that his parents were Seventh-day Adventists, but that he did not go to church or believe in it anymore. Having grown up with parents who were very strict churchgoers, Eric had become disillusioned.

Despite this fact, Eric's lifestyle and body language spoke volumes about his beliefs. What he refused to speak about verbally was undeniably revealed by his actions. Johnny had been drawn to Eric by his actions instead of his words.

Johnny asked his mentor, the pastor of the Friends Church (Quakers), about Seventh-day Adventists. Eventually, he decided to get a group of pastors together from as many different churches as he could. He wanted to ask all of them questions from the Bible.

Johnny was searching for a relationship with God. At some point, he had made a decision to follow Jesus, and he was now trying to find a Bible-based church with a direct, life-changing focus on the principles of God's love.

He set up the meeting and went with seven other art students to the Friends Church on a Thursday evening. A Catholic priest, two Mormons, a Lutheran, a Methodist, and a Seventh-day Adventist, plus the Friends pastor, all attended. In the end, the Seventh-day Adventist pastor was able to answer all the Bible questions with a basic knowledge of the Scriptures that showed special insight and understanding. In time, all seven of the art students would join the Seventh-day Adventist faith.

Eric noted that Pastor Ken from the local Seventh-day Adventist church started coming to the school each Friday afternoon to pray with Johnny's group, usually on the street corner in a circle. Eric was embarrassed by the whole thing, but he did like Pastor Ken. He was very kind and gentle, and completely unafraid of public opinion.

> For by grace ye are saved through faith; and that not of yourselves: it is the gift of God: Not of works, lest any man should boast.
>
> – Eph. 2: 8-9, KJV

CHAPTER 5

Sobering Surrealness

On a cold Saturday night in November, shortly after his sophomore year began, one of the wealthy art students invited Johnny to a party that he was throwing at his apartment. Johnny wanted Eric to go with him, but Eric hesitated.

Art department parties were always the same! He knew that everyone would get drunk, be gross, stay up all night, and then sleep all the next day. There would also be many drugs. If things got too loud, the neighbors would call the police, the police would find the drugs, and everyone would get their names in the paper and spend three days in jail. Still, because Johnny was a supportive friend and a good critic of his work, Eric decided to accompany him to the party.

When they stepped into the front room of this third-floor apartment, they encountered strange sights and sounds. Some people were dressed in costumes that made them look like birds. They got in Johnny and Eric's faces and made chirping sounds. Other students dressed in other types of costumes were milling around and talking.

Johnny saw one of his friends and they started talking. Eric stood by, feeling very much out of place. Most of these were people that Eric did not know. The smell of alcohol was strong, and he could tell that some students had already had too much to drink. He could also smell drug odors. After visiting with several students, he was tired of the dialogue and decided to sit down away from the din of conversation.

> **Suddenly, Eric had the strange feeling that she was about to jump!**

Starting down a hall, he noticed an open door on the right. It was probably a guest bedroom, and it appeared to be unoccupied. Next to a tall window that overlooked the street below was a large, old-fashioned easy chair. *It must be around 10:00 p.m.* he thought. *This is just what I need!* Leaving the door open, he sat on the chair and almost immediately fell asleep.

He must have slept for some time. The next thing he knew, a cold wind blew across his face. He was still half-asleep, so it took a bit of time to realize that the window had been opened. The light from the streetlamp appeared to be blocked by a strange, moving shape. As he became accustomed to the light, he saw that the moving shape was not a curtain or a broken blind, but a human.

The young woman seemed to be doing some sort of ballet, talking to herself. He could make out the repeated words, "He loves me, he loves me not." She was dressed only in tights and a thin T-shirt.

It seemed to Eric that she was leaning too far out of the window. In the next moment, it looked like she was going to fall. Suddenly, Eric had the strange feeling that she was about to jump! He lunged from the chair and grabbed her around the waist.

He just barely managed to move backward enough to keep both of them from falling three stories down to the sidewalk below. As they fell back into the room, Eric's last thought was, *She feels so light*, then he hit his head on the bed's footboard. Feeling instant pain and seeing stars, he went out like a light.

Eric came to in the early hours of the morning. He found himself lying where he had fallen. He could barely move. Nevertheless, after a while, he crawled to the big easy chair and pulled himself up into it.

The pain in the back of his neck was excruciating, and his vision was blurry. He tried to stand and then sat back down quickly. He tried again after waiting a few minutes. That did not work either. After sitting there for some time, he was able to get to his feet.

Eric looked around the room, trying to piece together what had happened. A girl was lying under the bed with her feet sticking out. On the bed were several people trying to sleep off hangovers from the night before. Eric started to remember. He needed to get out of there and go to his apartment. It had been a crazy night!

As he started to leave, he looked back into the main room, seeing bottles all over the place and bodies lying on the floor in strange positions. The thought crossed his mind that this was a surreal landscape … something that one of the surrealist painters might have painted.

He took the elevator to the first floor. As he closed the outside door behind him, he was returned to full alertness by the freezing temperature. He briskly walked the several blocks back to Third Street, but instead of heading toward his hotel, he turned right and went into Romano's sandwich shop. He needed a cup of coffee to keep his head from coming off his shoulders.

CHAPTER 6

Mrs. Romano's Daughter

Mrs. Romano was behind the counter, and she smiled at him as he walked up. As Eric told her his order, she said with a smile, "You don't look so good."

He told her briefly what had happened and his disappointment in himself for not following his intuition. "Thanks," Eric said when she gave him the coffee, then he went to sit down. As he sipped his coffee, his neck began to feel better.

A few minutes later, Mrs. Romano came up to his table and asked if she could sit down and speak with him. Eric was a bit surprised, but he said, "Of course."

She went on to tell Eric that she had been watching him for some time. She had noticed that he was not at all like the other, boisterous art students. He seemed to be very kind and humble. He did not swear or talk negatively about others. In addition, he always said "Yes ma'am" and "No ma'am" when he spoke to females. This, she said, showed respect.

As she was speaking, Eric realized that she was only partially correct. He swore under his breath, especially if he hit his finger with a hammer. He also was disrespectful to his elders sometimes. Eric remembered an incident from when he was still commuting. He had been driving behind a tractor on a one-lane road. It was supposed to be a shortcut to school, but he had been forced to drive at a snail's pace because of the farmer and got to school a half hour late. He had become quite angry with himself and the farmer, calling the man several names that he ought not to repeat. *Yeah, I know I have a temper*, he thought.

Mrs. Romano continued, "As you know, we live in a rough neighborhood. I worry about Monique more and more as she is getting older. And now the pimp in charge of the girls across the street is always watching her." She explained that Monique walked to the bus stop in the morning and returned from school at 5:00 in the evening. In the winter this was after dark, so she worried about her daughter being alone.

Eric knew from Junior that Mrs. Romano, her daughter, and her brother-in-law, Dalio, lived above their restaurant on the second floor. Mrs. Romano now said that she had always picked up Monique when her husband was still alive, but since his death two years before, she had to stay in the shop to serve customers. Even though Uncle Dalio had come to stay with them shortly after Mrs. Romano's husband's death, he was not able to take orders or work the register. He could only carry food from the kitchen to the guests. This made him very useful indeed, especially at the dinner hour, but he couldn't help with Monique.

"Eric," she said, "could you walk her back here from the bus stop after she gets out of school each weekday? You seem to show up here around 5:00 p.m., anyway. This would be a huge relief to me! I'm not asking you to do this for nothing. I'm willing to give you a free meal every time."

"Thank you, Mrs. Romano, for the vote of confidence," Eric said. "I will be happy to help."

"Thank you so much," Mrs. Romano said.

Eric smiled at her. She returned to the register, and Eric turned toward the window. Completely exhausted, he tried to gather himself for class.

Eric's profound respect for the opposite sex and his unique way of speaking and carrying himself piqued Monique's interest as well. On that particular morning, she knew Eric had a class that started at 7:30. That was also when her bus left for the high school from the corner of Spring and High Streets, right across from the art school. She didn't know if her mom had asked for Eric's help yet, but walking together to the bus stop this morning would give her time to talk with him alone. She stood waiting just outside the shop door. As Eric came out, she joined him on his brisk walk to school.

"Good morning, Eric," she said with a smile. "Thought I would walk with you today."

"Sure," he said, "it's nice to have company."

As they walked, she did most of the talking: about her school, the fact that she was not yet sure what she wanted to do in life, that her mom wanted her to take over the family business, and so on. They reached the bus stop at the end of Third Street on time.

"Well, this is it," he said as she stood in line to get on the bus. "Have a nice day. By the way, I'll meet you here tonight like your mom asked."

Eric had been a good listener, but Monique felt a little guilty for monopolizing the whole conversation. He waited while she stepped onto the bus, then she turned and waved as the door closed. The bus moved into the traffic. As she took her seat, she again looked back to where Eric had been standing, but he had vanished.

All she knew about Eric was that when he went to church, he went on Saturday; and he did not use bad language. He was an Adventist, whatever that was. But the fact that he was careful with words and seemed to be kind to everyone set him apart from most of her other friends.

Even though she was modest, her good looks and the way she dressed made her very attractive to young men her age. They were always very forward in their advances and were always asking her out. The few times that she accepted those invitations had not gone well.

She had not complied with their desires, and so the jocks at her school had gotten very pushy and mean. Monique had become the butt of jokes and name-calling (not all the students at her school were this way, only the in crowd).

Her mom had always said that she would prefer that Monique only date good Catholic young men who had been to Catholic school. And she did not want Monique hanging out with the coarse crowd around the neighborhood. In fact, her mom did not want her dating at all until she was sixteen or seventeen. But what was interesting was that her mom reacted to Eric in a way that was so unusual.

Monique was jarred back to reality as the bus stopped in front of her school. She got off, and when it pulled away, she felt her personal security go with it. She tried to keep her backpack close to her, more for protection than anything else. She ran into the rough crowd of students and was pushed and jostled as she moved toward the doors. She ducked low under groping hands and pressed forward with all her strength. She was able to free herself by twisting sideways. The door opened in front of her, and she was pushed through the entrance by the press of the crowd.

Monique and another girl were first in. Security police stood along the wall. Monique moved quickly down the hall and entered her classroom. She sat down, and soon the room filled with students. The teacher entered, and everyone listened as the in-class assignment was given. Monique realized that this was just another day at school, and her heart settled down to a more normal pace.

CHAPTER 7

A Portrait of Hatred

After he left Monique at the bus stop, Eric went to school and settled down to work. He loved the smell of oil paint! Whenever he entered the classroom, the odors of paint and canvas, mixed with the fresh scent of wooden stretchers, was the smell of home to Eric. He decided to stay at school through the lunch hour to organize his studio and his thoughts.

As a sophomore he was eligible to enter the winter student art exhibition. Various patrons of the arts in the area often bought the works that were accepted for the exhibition. News agencies showed up, and some students would be written up in the newspaper. Some even became quite well-known when they got out of school.

As he thought more about it, Eric decided he would need a job to help pay for his tuition and to buy extra art supplies. Meanwhile, he was nagged by the fact that he had not gone to church for such a long time. Johnny always asked him about it. Eric could not understand why he was so persistent, yet he felt guilty. He thought about Phillip as well. In a crazy way, Phillip had been influential in Eric's true conversion to Christ.

Eric remembered a very cold day that past February. Phillip had said he had to meet someone in midtown, and then he and Eric could go to the movies. "I'll even pay your way," he had said good-naturedly.

Eric was not much of a moviegoer but needed a break. On their way Phillip kept looking at his watch. He finally said, "We are going to have to walk faster." They picked up the pace and arrived at the destination only a minute or two late.

A car was parked at the curb just off Main Street. As soon as they got near it, the passenger door opened and a woman jumped out. She approached Phillip, swearing at him and saying he was worthless and no good. She got in his face and told him in no uncertain terms that she would meet him here at the same time tomorrow, and that if he did not have the money by then, "Somebody will find you and break your legs."

She said this so intensely and with such hatred that Eric was caught completely off guard. He had never met anyone with such a demeanor before. The woman headed back toward the car, and as the door opened, she looked back toward Phillip with true hatred in her expression. She got into the car, and it roared away, turning onto Main Street and disappearing in the stream of traffic.

 A woman jumped out of the car, swearing at Phillip and saying he was worthless and no good.

At that moment, Eric saw the difference between love and hate. He felt almost too stunned to speak. Phillip turned and started walking toward the theater. Later, Eric tried to talk to Phillip about it, but Phillip would not talk. He pieced together that the woman had been a drug dealer, but that was about it.

God had given Eric a look at selfish, arrogant evil. Finally, he realized exactly what he wanted: a close relationship with Jesus! All Eric wanted was the love that Jesus had. For him, there was no other way.

Eric came out of his thoughts as he finished his studio organization, then left to meet Monique at the bus stop.

CHAPTER 8

Running a Gauntlet

Each day, Eric worked hard at school. His goal was to stay focused, so he took life drawing classes in the morning and painting in the afternoon. He also wanted to help the Romanos, but he realized after a while that he was not just walking Monique home from school. He also had to be very watchful. At that time of day, there were drunken sailors and art students who were very forceful and pushy. What could he do if one of these sailors grabbed Monique and tried to assault her? Then there were the pimps and drunks that seemed to appear from nowhere as the evening progressed. The police were on the street, but through the noise and din of the crowd, it would be impossible to get them to notice two students.

Eric felt that maybe he had bitten off more than he could chew. He did not know what to do! Trying to keep track of a beautiful young woman, who would appear very desirable to most of these men on the street, was a huge task. He would never be able to focus on school unless he could resolve this situation. Then he remembered Psalm 22:5, which stated, "They cried unto thee, and were delivered: they trusted in thee, and were not confounded."

Since he had left home, Eric had prayed about every hurdle he had to jump (he had never stopped, since he did not equate prayer with church at all). He decided that prayer was what he would rely on with this, too. Not long after, as he stood at the bus stop waiting for Monique one Monday, he had come up with a couple of possible solutions.

As she got off the bus, she smiled good-naturedly. They turned the corner onto Third Street. There was a group of students standing in front of an antique shop, so Eric directed Monique into the group. He acted as if he was interested in their conversation, and as the group moved down the street, he and Monique stayed near the middle and moved with them. After about fifteen minutes, they found themselves in front of Romano's. This option would not always work, but it had this time! Eric decided that next time he would have her wear a hood so she would have a disguise.

They stepped into the shop, where most of the tables were full. Mrs. Romano smiled at both of them as they approached the register. "Your meals are ready. You can eat in the back." Monique showed the way. They went through the hanging curtain behind the register and entered a small, tidy room. Two small windows overlooked an alley between the building complexes. A little table with two chairs sat in front of one of the windows, with two plates of food ready to eat.

Monique quickly went to the chair on the left and sat down. Eric took the other. Monique ate her sandwich as if she had not eaten in a very long time. Eric bowed his head and made a silent prayer for the girl sitting across from him and also asked God to bless the food.

Eric looked up. Monique had stopped eating and was looking at him. He smiled, then they ate together quietly, as if they were both deep in their own thoughts. Eric had not been around girls much, so he was a bit shy. Monique was different: it was not that she was shy, she only seemed to be respectful of his space.

As soon as he had finished, Eric got up and took his plate to a sink that had other dishes in it. He rinsed his off, said, "Catch you tomorrow," and walked through the curtain back into the shop. It was still crowded with students from several schools. Everyone was talking and seemed to be having a good time. Eric decided he would go back to school and work until 11:00 p.m., but as he started to step through the shop door, he felt a soft touch on his arm. He turned to see Monique.

"My mother wants to talk to you," she said. "It will only take a minute."

He looked back into the shop to where Mrs. Romano was. Monique pulled him by the arm, so he followed her to the end of the counter, away from the register, where Mrs. Romano passed a bag to him.

"Here, I wanted to send you with something to snack on," she said with a smile.

"Thank you," Eric said, and turned to go.

She called after him, "Careful on the street!"

CHAPTER 9

The Joy and Peril of Good Painting

Eric took his first watercolor class in the spring of his sophomore year. Of the many assignments that were given, he enjoyed going to the salvage yard the most. The salvage yard bordered the ocean and mostly contained industrial machines, long chains from ocean liners, and even huge anchors. There were also many antique train parts like couplers and iron rails. Everything was oversized and fun to draw.

One day Eric and his Catholic friend Bill went there to paint. Eric decided to paint a picture of fishing boats with various large objects as framing. He sat between a huge anchor and a broken-down dynamo, with a pile of railroad ties in the foreground. Beyond the ties were the ocean and the fishing boats. The foreground was a silhouette to the middle and background.

When he and Bill ate their lunches, they fed the seagulls and talked about the sea; how the ocean and the smell of the tide flats were so much a part of their surroundings. As the tide went out, they could see what was left of an old schooner. The keel lay in the mud, and its ribs were rotted to the mud line, but its skeletal shape was still visible. Many such schooners were built in Bath, Maine, or Wiscasset. They were the workhorses of the New England coast.

Eric was able to complete most of his painting before the sun went down. He did not realize it at the time, but it would become one of his best that semester.

After a great day they were ready to head back. They were careful to carry their freshly painted artworks so as not to smudge the surfaces until they were completely dry. After reaching the school, Eric and Bill went to their individual studio spaces and set the paintings up on easels so they were ready for the next class, which would be a critique.

Unfortunately, rumors were circulating about this particular watercolor teacher that bothered Eric and many of the other younger art students. Some had accused him of stealing their works. His excuse was always that his dog had eaten their work, and he would apologize profusely. Nevertheless, students became very leery … especially after seeing their work at a gallery with the teacher's name on it and a $100.00 price tag! However, the fact that this teacher was such a good teacher otherwise made it hard for students to complain too much.

They finished their paintings the following day, and when critique day came, Eric and Bill received good reviews; the teacher accepted their work as finished. All the same, Eric did not turn in his painting from the salvage yard. Instead, he turned in another work that was not as good but which had also passed the critique. He ended up doing this each time he had an assignment in that class with that teacher.

CHAPTER 10

Nightlife

That same night, Eric left the studio and started back to his hotel at around 11:30 p.m. There was a steady stream of traffic moving down Third Street on both sides, but now the atmosphere was more business-like.

Across from where he was walking, a large black car was parked in the shadows. Eric could see cigarette smoke moving upward from a partly-opened car window. Suddenly, the passenger door flew open and a large, dark figure dressed in a heavy coat lunged onto the sidewalk. Eric recognized him as one of the bodybuilders from his old roommate's boxing days. The man strode toward a group of girls standing together next to the curb and yelled something at one of them.

The girl started to back away toward the side of the building. He slapped her across the face before she could move out of reach. She fell backward against the wall and landed in a heap on the sidewalk. He proceeded to kick her several times. Then he abruptly turned and strode back to the car.

The group of girls had disappeared. No one else got in the man's way. Eric was very disturbed, to say the least! What really bothered him was that no one had even tried to come to the girl's aid. Eric stayed in the shadows a long time before he continued down the street to his apartment.

When he passed by Romano's, the place was dark. Further on, Bobbie was not in her window. Luce, however, was in hers, talking to two sailors in the street below. Eric walked in the dark shadows until the crossroads in front of the old hotel. Then he crossed the street and started up the steep steps leading to the beautiful Victorian doorway where all the hotel guests entered.

About halfway up, he smelled the strong odor of alcohol mixed with the stench of urine. He looked into the shadows at the base of the building and saw six men passing a bottle. One would take a swallow, then another, until it had completed the rounds. The smell turned Eric's stomach, and he ran the rest of the way up the steps and into the hotel lobby. One of the old alcoholics yelled something at him, but he could not tell what.

> On Eric's bed was a man dressed only in his underwear, moaning and groaning. He must have wandered in.

The lobby was packed with people. Eric could see Junior talking to a couple of new guests. The bellhop seemed to be very busy as well. A tall woman was dressed in a white fur coat and held a cigarette holder with a lit cigarette. She had a short, little man in tow. He was drunk and had difficulty making his way up the stairs. She had to hold onto his arm to keep him from staggering backward. Eric walked around several groups of people to get his mail from the office. Without a word, Junior handed him a single letter.

Eric was tired of the din and the sound of strained voices. He put his mail into a bag of rolls that Mrs. Romano had given him that day and headed up the stairs to the second floor. After a short walk down the corridor, he came to his room and unlocked the door. When he turned on the light, he was met with a horrible scene and smell.

On Eric's bed was a man dressed only in his underwear, moaning and groaning. He must have wandered in through the small back door to the bathroom that Eric shared with a guest across the hall; he had apparently forgotten to lock the door. Eric recognized the man. He lived on the third floor with his brother. Both were prone to fighting, and both were drunk most of the time.

Now what? he thought. *How am I going to get him out of the room?* He decided to see if Junior could do something. Eric closed his door and quickly went back downstairs. Peeking inside Junior's cubbyhole office, he saw the second-in-command sitting at the desk.

Eric asked, "Where is Junior?"

"He's gone to the store," he said. "He'll be gone for about twenty minutes."

Eric quickly said "Thanks," then returned upstairs to his room, wondering what to do next. He was surprised to find his bed empty and the door to the bathroom wide open. Eric walked over and looked inside. The floor was covered with vomit and shards of glass, and cold air was pouring in from outside. Stepping gingerly toward the shattered window, Eric saw the man on a pile of bricks below. He had fallen from the second floor!

The man sat up and started to crawl. Suddenly, he stood up and slid down to the parking lot pavement. *Any sober person would have been badly hurt by the fall, or killed,* Eric thought. The man slowly walked down the alley.

Eric left the bathroom and latched the door behind him. He sat on the edge of the bed and wrote out a report for Junior on what he thought had happened. He ran down to the office and left the note on Junior's desk.

Back upstairs, his room did not seem to be very messed up. The only thing that appeared out of place was his easel. It had been knocked over with the canvas on it facing down. Unfortunately, upon closer inspection, he saw a tear in the canvas from one side to the other. Still, it was now after midnight, and Eric was too exhausted after everything that had happened to do more, so he fell into bed. He was asleep almost immediately.

Wow, he thought when he awoke, *what time is it?* He got up and pulled open the shade. Bright sunlight came pouring into his room. His small wall clock read 10:30 a.m. Eric caught his breath. He had already missed one class and was about to miss another! He quickly put on a clean shirt, then he walked carefully into the bathroom—around the broken glass littering the floor—and splashed cold water on his face. Then he went back into his room and looked into the mirror. What he saw was not great.

Eric locked his door behind him and ran downstairs. Junior was not at his desk and the lobby was almost empty. For some reason, he always felt uneasy when Junior was not present. He walked quickly down the street. The shops were all open, so he stopped to buy a bagel and cream cheese. Then he caught a glimpse of Bobbie getting into the back seat of a black sedan parked in front of her apartment. The door closed behind her and the car headed north, gathering speed as it went.

Where is she being taken? Eric thought. Bobbie seemed so callous, yet something told him she had a completely different side, especially since that conversation when she had shown him an attitude 180 degrees different from usual. He continued toward school, eating his bagel and deep in thought. He told himself to focus on school and stop worrying about forty-something prostitutes.

Class went well. It was a day to work on sculpture and drawing. His sculpture teacher only came to class to critique once a week, but he was very good and helpful. Eric had been working on an alabaster figure for over a month. It was frustrating because the stone in one of the figure's legs had cracked, but because of his teacher's guidance that day, Eric learned how to fix the figure, and much of his frustration disappeared.

CHAPTER 11

Traffic and Accidents

5:00 p.m. always came all too quickly. Once again, Eric was back on the busy street waiting for Monique's bus. However, today something was holding it up. He could hear cars honking and people shouting. Eric jogged up the street to see what it was.

He pushed his way through the crowd and saw Michael, one of the most talented art students, sitting in an easy chair in the center of the street. He was painting a picture on a short easel while traffic rushed by on either side. The police were trying to talk to him. Finally, two officers picked him up in the chair and set him on the sidewalk. Another brought his easel. He simply kept on painting as if nothing had happened. This was typical of Michael.

Eric trotted back to the bus stop. Monique had by now arrived and was standing against the side of the building, waiting. She smiled a greeting, and they turned and started down Third Street. She put the hood of her jacket over her head, and they walked in silence. After about five minutes, they stopped near a warehouse entrance because a large, covered truck was coming out.

Suddenly, as the driver turned into the traffic, he swerved up onto the sidewalk. Eric lunged and knocked Monique back against the building. He fell to his knees as he pushed up against the wall, scraping both kneecaps and bruising his elbow.

Monique sat on the sidewalk, looking around as if trying to figure out what had just happened. He had pushed her pretty hard. Eric asked, "Are you okay? I hope I didn't hurt you. That was a very narrow escape. He almost ran us down."

Monique nodded slowly.

Eric helped her get up and asked her again, "Are you hurt?"

"I don't think so," she said quietly.

"Well, let's get you home," he said.

Bruised and stiff, they walked to the sandwich shop as quickly as they could. The place was crowded, and Monique went to the back. Eric was lucky enough to find a table with one chair in the shop's back corner. He slumped into the seat and put his head down. He felt pain in his knees and his wrists. After a few minutes, he seemed to be better. He straightened up.

He looked toward the counter and saw Uncle Dalio bringing out meals while Mrs. Romano took orders from a line of customers. Eric got in line, but after a few minutes, he realized it was going to take too long to get food. He retraced his steps to get his jacket from the table, and saw someone else sitting there. He was about to say something when the person turned toward him. To his surprise, it was Monique. She had changed clothes and brought sandwiches.

Before he could say anything, she said, "My mom prepared this in advance for us. Oh! Look at you. You are bleeding."

He looked around, mystified.

"It's your knee!" she said. "Your left one is bleeding."

Eric noticed the tear and stains on his pant leg for the first time. It hurt, but he said, "Well, it doesn't hurt much now. I think it will be okay. How are you feeling?"

She responded, "One elbow has a small cut, and both my wrists are complaining, but I think I will live."

Traffic and Accidents

They ate their sandwiches and made small talk about the day. After the better part of an hour, Eric stood up from the table. He told Monique that he had to go. "I'm going to be drawing from life this evening," he said. "I have to draw people that are going about their everyday work. Everyone has to be in motion."

Monique asked. "Isn't it hard to draw people that are moving?"

"It takes a lot of patience," Eric said. "By using multiple outlines, it gives a sense of movement. It's like when you move the camera while taking a picture. When things look fuzzy, it only means that you have moved the camera.

"Thanks for bringing the sandwiches, Monique," he continued. "Tell your mom that I appreciate her thoughtfulness."

Then a voice behind him said, "She doesn't have to tell her mom. You can tell her yourself."

Eric turned and saw Mrs. Romano smiling at him. He felt a little embarrassed.

"Oh," he said, "I just wanted to thank you for the meal."

"You are certainly welcome," she replied. "Monique mentioned what happened, and I just wanted to thank *you* for saving my daughter from getting hurt or killed. I think I know who that driver was," she said, "and I don't think that near miss was accidental."

Mrs. Romano paused. "Maybe I had better tell you about some things that went on in the past and are still going on," she said. "I will tell you what I know to be the truth, and then I will tell you some hearsay. Eventually, you will have to make up your own mind."

Both Monique and her mom were looking at Eric intently. "Well, I guess you'd better fill me in," he said.

Mrs. Romano nodded. "Some years ago, my husband worked for a large trucking company in the city. His job was to load boxes onto trucks with a forklift. The dispatcher would tell him what to load and how much.

"One day, while he was lifting some boxes of pet food high onto a shelf, the shelf gave way under the weight of the boxes and everything fell to the concrete floor. The boxes broke open, but instead of having dog food in them, they were loaded with handguns and bags of white, powder-like material.

"Too late, my husband recognized what it was. Someone was watching and rushed up to throw a tarp over the goods. Then he yelled at my husband and told him to go to the office. There he was told to wait.

"After what seemed like a very long time, two men entered the room. They began to ask him questions about what he had seen. He explained in as much detail as he could remember. When he had finished, he was told he could leave. Later my husband confided in me that, for the first time in his life, he was scared.

"As the months went by, little things seemed to go wrong every day. After several of these incidents, my husband and I talked it over. We decided that he would try to find a different job with a different company, so he gave his two-week notice. That morning was the last time I saw my husband alive!

"I was told that he had gotten off the forklift to tighten a rope around a large, heavy pallet. Somehow the forklift went into gear and pinned him against the wall. He was quickly taken to a hospital but was found to be dead upon arrival."

As Mrs. Romano was telling the story, her eyes filled with tears. Monique put her arm around her mother's shoulders and embraced her.

"I'm sorry," said Eric. "I'm so sorry, Mrs. Romano."

She brushed her eyes with the back of her hand and gave a small smile. She continued to speak. "Uncle Dalio worked for the same company. After my husband's death, Dalio also complained to me about small things going wrong. He was worried that he too might have a serious accident. Then one day, it happened.

"He was high up on a scaffold doing some electrical work. The scaffold let go, and he fell two stories. Through an act of God, he survived the fall. However, he hit his head and received a serious concussion. After several weeks he was able to come home from the hospital, but he was never the same; he was permanently damaged by the fall. He can function, but the things he can do are limited. Though he is only a shell of his former self, he is a help to us, and we love him. Eric, I'm telling you this because things are not always what they seem around here. I think that my husband's death was not an accident and that Dalio's accident was also planned.

"There are things going on here that no one wants to talk about. It appears a sort of mob is active here. They pressure local businesses to buy products from specific companies, many of which are not local. For example, we here at the sandwich shop are pressured to buy our paper products from one particular place. They try to force out those that don't comply with their program. There have been several other 'accidents' recently. We don't know what kind of trouble we will run into in the future.

> There are things going on here that no one wants to talk about.

"Drugs are another issue. For example, 'The company,' as people sometimes call it, offers rides to kids walking home from school. They take them to parties and give them brownies laced with marijuana or hand out other drugs like heroin, LSD, and cocaine. They do this until the kids become hooked, then they start charging them for the drugs. You have probably seen a van let kids out in your neighborhood; they walk carelessly down the street, faces flushed, hitting road signs, kicking the sides of cars, or tearing things up in general."

Eric remembered having seen this happen several times. He hadn't been sure at the time what he was witnessing, but it certainly wasn't good.

Mrs. Romano had finished speaking. Eric decided to ask her about Bobbie. "Across from here, there are two old streetwalkers calling down to almost every male that walks by; Bobbie and Luce. Who are they? How come they can be so loud and fill the air with such profanity?"

Mrs. Romano and Monique exchanged glances. "That's the company, too," Mrs. Romano said. Apparently those girls are carefully regulated and punished if they don't follow their wishes. They are two of the older generation of streetwalkers who have been here for about ten years. They have been doing it for so long that even the police just shrug their shoulders and walk the other way.

"From what I have witnessed and gathered from others, the older one, Bobbie, started here first. The company picked her up almost immediately as she was very good-looking and had a personality that fit her profession. She became a high-paid escort. She had a chauffeur and wore furs of high quality. But eventually, she became too old for that. She was allowed by the company to have that little room on the second floor across from us. The other woman showed up about five years ago. Like Bobbie, she stuck out. She wasn't as pretty, but she had a quick wit. She seemed to become a regular with the company's executives."

Eric had many more questions, but he decided to hold those for another time. He had been listening for over an hour, and he knew that he had to go back to school. "Well," he said, "thank you for filling me in. This has answered many of the questions I had about Third Street. I am worried that I cannot protect Monique from any real danger. However, I'm a praying person, so I have asked God to keep her safe and help me to do the job you have asked me to do."

Mrs. Romano smiled. "I think you're doing just fine. Today was enough to show me that my intuition about you is not wrong."

Eric felt his face getting red as Mrs. Romano continued, "Until you came, I would lay awake at night worrying. Now I'm able to sleep through the whole night. So you see, prayers *have* been answered."

Eric smiled sheepishly and said, "I've got to go." He nodded to Monique and said, "See you tomorrow at 5:00 p.m." Without waiting for a response, he left the shop.

CHAPTER 12

Sketching Bobbie Again

On the street, a blast of cold air hit him. Bobbie was advertising again, so even though it was quite cold, he decided to do some sketching. He wanted to capture her as she gestured and shouted at passers-by.

A small group that looked like students moved closer, so he joined them walking down the street. The streetlamps lit up everything except the darkest corners. As he got to a dark area, he slipped into the shadows and sat down on the concrete to draw.

Bobbie was wearing a red dress with a thin sweater. As usual, she was gesturing to the men walking below. She would make fun of any couple, saying, "Hey, darlin', she can't do for you what I can. She looks too skinny and small." Then she would use expletives, causing the couple to walk quickly out of earshot, only to be surrounded by a group of younger women farther down the street.

Eric found it difficult to focus on his drawing; partly because his fingers were so cold and partly because he was preoccupied with what

Mrs. Romano had related to him. He was beginning to see that the world was a truly messed-up place. He thought about Uncle Dalio—no doubt a very good person—and how other people who wanted to make sure their lies were not found out had forever changed his life.

Eric got up abruptly. He did not realize, being so deep in thought, that he had been staring at Bobbie. As he moved out of the shadows, they locked eyes for the first time. He turned away quickly and moved off down the street at full stride. He heard her say something, but he felt too embarrassed to answer. When he reached the end of Third Street, he quickly crossed the intersection and ran up the steps of the hotel. The old winos were nowhere in sight.

When he went by the office to pick up his mail, Junior motioned for him to come around behind the desk. Junior almost never had anything to say, so Eric was surprised at this attention.

Junior asked, "Eric, what do you know about the broken window in the bathroom?"

Eric said, "I left you a note explaining what happened. Did you get it?"

"Yeah, but Mr. Jones wanted me to get more details if I could. He would like to collect insurance since the window and part of the sill are broken."

Eric reiterated the events the way he had figured them out.

Then Junior said, "Mr. Jones was wondering why there was a trail of blood going from the bathroom into your room."

Eric was surprised. "Wow, I didn't see that."

"Ok," said Junior, "I will relay to Mr. Jones what you said. In the future, keep your door closed. The two brothers on the third floor are very dangerous when they are drinking. Almost every night, they fight with each other, and I am trying to keep our other guests from being harmed."

"Thanks, Junior. I'll keep my head up and my eyes peeled."

Junior smiled, "OK, Eric. Here's your mail. See you."

Eric headed toward the stairs. Tonight, when he opened his door, everything looked normal. Again, he was too tired to remove his clothes. He pulled a blanket over himself and immediately fell asleep. Morning came very early, but he was able to get up and get dressed, and he still had time to eat breakfast.

Beside his bed, in the small closet where his clothes hung, was a shelf. His breakfast material, consisting of two boxes of cereal and a box of raisins, was there. He also had paper plates, plastic forks, spoons, and a roll of paper towels. Eric made his meal, and as he finished, he noticed that the sun was shining outside. It was another cold, clear day with vestiges of snow.

It was almost 8:00 a.m. The lobby was empty except for Junior, who waved briefly as Eric passed by. He ran up to the large, double doors and pushed the right side open, bounding down the steps and onto the street. He expected the cold blast of air, but it still took his breath away momentarily. He decided to jog to school to keep warm. He felt better today than he had for a long time. As he ran, Eric found himself whistling.

CHAPTER 13

Pastoral Scene

The weeks went by quicker than he realized. Soon, Eric was making plans to go home for Thanksgiving. It would be his first time seeing his parents in almost two years!

Eric thought back to when he had left the first time. Things had not gone well. His parents had not been at all interested in him going to a non-Adventist institution. They were second-generation Adventists and had developed many traditional points of view. First, they did not want him to marry a non-Adventist Christian. Second, they thought he was too young to be on his own in a big city. Third, they thought he might get into drugs and start drinking and smoking. These were real possibilities!

Eric's dad had said, "Your argument for going to that art school is that there is no art school in our church. However, it's not even a Christian school. I don't think you're ready for that kind of worldly environment … you have always gone to church school!"

Eric told him, "I'm not going to a college where there are no art professionals! I have chosen to be an artist, and this is the closest art school."

His mom said, "If he hasn't got our values by this time, then I don't think we can do more than we already have. I guess I just don't want him to go away so young. He isn't ready."

Dad answered, "Well, I don't know what we're going to do. As it is, Eric has already spent all summer with his uncle, who doesn't believe in God. It's no wonder that he is going into the world."

Mom said, "Maybe our fears will not be realized. He is very talented and may do well in that environment. He will go anyway, even if we do not help. I think we *can* help, and eventually he will see that we were supportive."

While they argued Eric had gone out, gotten into his car, and left. He had driven around for a while just thinking. He felt like he had been put in a box and was not allowed to try anything outside of that box. *I haven't had a chance to test the water*, he thought.

Now as Thanksgiving approached, Eric thought this was a good opportunity to have a reunion and try to get back into his parents' good graces. He asked his good friend Joe to go with him. They both loved the sea and sailing ships. In painting class, they both painted seascapes and spent time drawing fishing boats at the dock in the harbor near the art school. They could make it a ski vacation.

His parents took to Joe immediately. He was good at conversation, had a quick sense of humor, and a smile to match. It turned out Joe and Eric's dad both loved insects.

"Wow, you never told me that your dad had such a beautiful insect collection! How come?" Joe said with a smile.

Eric responded, "I didn't know you were that interested, or I would have said something."

While Joe and Eric's dad looked at beetles that had been collected in Japan before the bombing of Hiroshima, Eric thought again about his childhood.

He had always been a little bit different; he never quite fit in. He had always gone to church with his mom and always went to church school, but Eric seemed to always be in trouble. He was liked by most of the kids, but he didn't seem to have any real friends. Perhaps it was because he was shy. The girls in particular seemed to shy away from him, except for his cousins.

As a student in grade school, he was a little less than average. He just didn't like school. He had decided quite early on that he wanted to be an artist. He loved to draw and paint. His mother and uncle were also talented. Eric's mother drew cartoon characters, and Uncle George sang; even at times on the local radio station.

It was easy for others to see he had talent. His mother would supply him with paints, brushes, pencils, and plenty of drawing paper; and all his teachers patted him on the back for that skill. But he had no discipline for other studies. He was always interested in the outdoors. Weekends were spent in nature observing frogs, rabbits, and other small animals.

In high school, his teachers didn't think he was "college material." Even though he had gotten some A's, he was not considered smart enough. So Eric thought that art school would be the best place for him. In fact, it was Joe, who was now having such a fun time with Eric's parents, who had suggested to him to come.

The day of that big fight before he started art school, after thinking for a while in the car, Eric had gone back home. His parents' argument was still going on, and he overheard some of it. He heard her quote from Psalm 5:11: "But let all those that put their trust in thee rejoice: let them ever shout for joy, because thou defendest them." His mom was definitely more on his side.

Throughout his life, Eric's mom had emphasized different Bible texts, especially the Psalms, to help him overcome the hurdles of life. Psalm 5:11 and 12 was one she'd told him often. She always prayed that he would put his trust in God.

He also heard her tell his dad, "It will kill him if we try to cram him into our box. He has always been on the outside. Like you, he's a loner; very independent. He doesn't follow the crowd."

Dad said, "Well, if anything goes wrong, it will be your fault!" Then he slammed the door and stormed out of the house.

Eric had concluded that day that he only believed in God because his parents did. *What if it is all a big lie?* he had wondered. Everyone talked about having faith to believe. Well, for him, it was all up in the air. How did he know that God really existed? He felt like his parents did not want him to know about the reality of life. However, in the end, they had both agreed Eric should go to art school. The day he left, driving six hours to school, life, as he saw it, was just beginning!

In the present, Joe and his dad were laughing loudly over something Joe had said. Eric had never heard his dad laugh like that! His father had always been stern and self-centered. Eric began to realize that perhaps *he* was self-centered, too.

That night after dinner, when Joe volunteered to help clean up the kitchen, Eric seized his chance. He got his dad's attention, and they moved quietly into the living room.

"Dad," Eric began, "I know I've been distant and resentful. I've avoided you and mom since I left. But I'm starting to see things differently since I went away to school. I know you only wanted what was best for me. I'm sorry, and I love you."

> "You are a diamond in the rough, and life has a way of polishing a diamond," Mom said.

Eric's dad smiled and drew him into a hug, then they went to help the others.

Eric and Joe managed to go skiing at Mount Sunapee only once. The skiing was not good due to the lack of snow. When Thanksgiving break ended, before they headed back to school, Eric's mother talked to him.

"I wish you'd be in touch more," she said. "I wonder how you're doing."

"I know," Eric said. "I'm sorry, Mom. I'll do better. I'm still figuring things out, but I realize more and more how much your love and influence mean to me."

"You know," she said, "It's like I always said: you are a diamond in the rough, and life has a way of polishing a diamond." Mom cried as she gave him a hug goodbye. As Eric turned to go, she said, "I'll pray that you will find what you are looking for."

CHAPTER 14

A Warning and Grace

It was Monday morning and very cold when they started back. The sun came up, and the temperature warmed up enough so that the ice pretty much turned to slush, but the roads were still a little icy. After about three hours of driving, they stopped to get a cup of coffee at a small café that served breakfast all day.

"Hey, let's get an egg on toast with sausage," said Joe. "I'm starved"

Eric replied, "OK, but we need to make it quick; I don't want to get back too late. I have an early morning class tomorrow."

The waitress came to the table to take their order. She seemed nice. Eric guessed she was about thirty years old. Most women her age wore quite short skirts, but hers was unusually modest.

She asked Eric with a smile, "Are you sure you wouldn't like some breakfast, too? It won't take long."

"No, thank you. Just bring me coffee," Eric responded. "We are in a hurry."

She had a kind but wistful look on her face as she went to the back to put in their orders. She came back after about ten minutes. "Here you are," she said, "Enjoy." She walked a little distance and abruptly turned back to the table. "You're sure you don't want something to eat?"

"No, thanks," Eric said.

She had that strange look on her face again. Eric was not trying to be unkind, but her actions began to give him an uneasy feeling. Joe took only a short time to eat, but to Eric it seemed much longer.

As they got up from the table to leave, the waitress came back with coffee. "Please … please have another cup."

This time Joe told her, "Got to be going. No thanks."

Eric had opened the door and was about to step outside when he felt a light touch on his arm. "Just one more cup." She almost seemed to be begging.

Eric said, "No, *thanks!*" with more emphasis this time. He closed the door quickly and bolted down the steps to his car.

Joe was already sitting in the front passenger seat. He smiled good-naturedly and said, "What took you so long?"

Eric rolled his eyes, started the car, and backed out of the parking space. He looked in his rearview mirror at the café. The waitress was still standing behind the doorway, her hand upon the glass, looking directly at him. Now, this made him feel much more uneasy than before. He thought to himself, *Am I imagining all of this?* They pulled out onto the highway and headed east.

Home was still over three hours away. It seemed as if Joe had dozed off. Usually, he couldn't stop talking. After about five miles, Eric turned on the radio. Then it happened.

They started around a wide curve in the road when a large touring car met them head-on. No one had time to react. All Eric saw were fine glass crystals floating toward his face and eyes ... then he was out like a light.

When he awoke he heard the sound of fluid dripping. It smelled like antifreeze. He tried to move, but the steering wheel was pinning him to his seat. He could not move his right arm. His left arm seemed to be okay, though. He bent his neck to look at Joe.

Joe appeared to be unconscious. He had a deep cut on his forehead. As Eric looked, Joe started to shake uncontrollably. *I've got to free myself*, he thought, *and get Joe out.*

His knees now began to throb. Eric could see that the knobs on the dash had punctured them both. He finally shoved the door open with his one good arm, and after some maneuvering he got himself out of the car. He was able to pull Joe out of his seat and get him to the pavement.

Joe drifted in and out of consciousness. Eric pulled him to his feet, but every time he started to walk with Joe, Joe went limp. Finally, they got to a spot in the field near the car where there was no snow, and he set Joe down. He got Joe's coat from the back seat and wrapped him in it.

Joe was able to speak for the first time. "Man, what happened?"

Eric didn't answer. He walked as fast as he could to the other car. Where his knees had been punctured, he had a great deal of pain. His right arm was useless. He reached the vehicle and tried to open the door, but it was jammed shut. The driver was an older man with white hair. He was pinned in by the steering wheel. It looked like he had bumped his head as well. He was trying to say something, but Eric couldn't make it out.

Someone must have called the state police because as Eric was heading back to Joe, he could hear the siren. The police arrived in a short time; the ambulance appeared as well. They had to cut the door of the second vehicle off with a torch to get the older man out of the car. Both cars were totaled beyond recognition.

Eric and Joe were moved into the ambulance. Neither of them said anything to the other. It was hard for Eric to get the waitress out of his mind. If they had just spent five more minutes in the café, this would not have happened! The thought crossed his mind that she was his guardian angel, warning him. He, Joe, and the elderly man were taken to the hospital. After an hour or two Eric and Joe were released.

Joe called a friend of his to come pick them up. While waiting, they had time to recoup a little. Joe had a bandage around his head just above his eyes all the way around the back. Both of Eric's knees were bandaged and his arm was in a sling. It had mostly stopped hurting, but it still throbbed a little. Over the next several days, his arm would remain very stiff, and he would have to try to draw with his left hand.

While they were sitting in the waiting room in the hospital, the elderly man came out through the double doors of the emergency room and walked over to them, smiling. Under his shirt and jacket, he had a large bandage. He introduced himself.

"My name is Mr. Sanders. I am sorry that we had to meet this way. Thanks for trying to help me back there on the highway."

"I heard you boys were not badly hurt. I have three cracked ribs, but the doctor said there was nothing else wrong." He gave each of them his business card. "If there is anything I can do for you, just call me at this number." He shook hands with them warmly. "Goodbye," he said, and walked out the front door of the hospital to a waiting cab.

God is our refuge and strength, a very present help in trouble. Therefore will not we fear, though the earth be removed, and though the mountains be carried into the midst of the sea. Psalm 46:1-2

After Joe's friend picked them up, they went to the local garage where their car had been towed to pick up their luggage and skis. The rest of the trip back to school was uneventful. They dropped Eric off at his hotel first and then went on to Joe's home. Eric finally got to bed at 4:00 a.m. His thoughts returned to that waitress. Even though he had not heeded God's warning, He had saved Eric's life again!

CHAPTER 15

Surprising Encounters

Before he knew it, the Christmas season had arrived. All his friends went home, but the Romanos invited him to eat with them. They were going to have their meal at noon, and then they were taking a bus to a relative's house for an evening get-together with family. But Eric had eaten the noon meal with the Romanos for several months now, and he wanted to give them a rest.

Then Connie, one of the models from his life drawing class, invited a group of students over to her apartment for a party. Parties weren't his thing, but he liked her as a friend and she seemed to hang around a group of good students. He decided to go for companionship. Ultimately, he wouldn't be alone!

It was dark out when he arrived, but she met him at the door with a welcoming smile and ushered him into a brightly lit hallway. She brought him to a cozy, tastefully-decorated living room. The heavy curtains had been pulled closed since the apartment was on the ground floor. Connie said, "Make yourself at home. I'm still in the process of preparing the food. So far, you are the only one who has shown up." She smiled sweetly and left the room.

He could hear pots and pans rattling down the hall, and Connie was singing to herself. He sat in front of the gas-log fire, feeling warm and not too lonely after all. After about ten minutes, she returned to tell Eric the food was ready. She had changed into what looked like pajamas and seemed a little preoccupied with something.

As they entered a small dining area, he could smell turkey and stuffing. She had set a table for two with goblets and napkin rings. He also noticed that there was a bottle of wine on ice. He got the distinct impression that she had planned this for just the two of them. Then he thought, *Why would she do that?* Connie was his age and quite pretty, but he had never felt that there was anything between them. She had always been nice, but nothing else.

They sat down together, and Eric prayed for the meal. Connie uncovered the small, metal pans, and they began to eat. The meal consisted of sliced turkey and stuffing, cranberries, and sweet potatoes in a sweet sauce.

Eric thought to himself, *This is a very pleasant evening.* He was really beginning to relax as she served the wine. Though Eric didn't usually drink, he decided to humor her. After eating, they moved back into the living room, and Connie began to talk about her job as a model.

Eric was curious. Art school was the first time he had seen a nude woman in real life. He had always been taught that seeing a woman unclothed outside of marriage was evil; that you should hide yourself and get away from the scene as soon as possible, trying not to even think about what you saw! He had many questions.

He asked Connie, "What is it like to stand naked in front of a group of people you don't know? How do you move so beautifully from one pose to another so that it is almost imperceptible to see the transition? How do you maintain a pose without moving for thirty minutes, with only a one-minute break after fifteen minutes?"

Connie responded, "First, I would like to share something: modeling is a real job. To do it well, you must be in excellent physical condition. I have worked very hard at it because it's about the only job I can get that pays this much. Plus, I like the hours. It's only part-time, so I have the flexibility to do my studies.

"The other thing that I really like is that I can use some of my ballet training as I transition from one pose to the next. You have noticed some of those moves.

"To answer your other question, I have had to practice … a lot. After a while, it becomes much easier to stay in one position."

Then Connie said, "I have a question for you, Eric. Where are you from, and what makes you so darn nice to people?"

Eric was taken aback. Fortunately, the light was low, so she couldn't see the expression on his face.

"I'm from a small town in the center of New Hampshire," he said, "next to Vermont. I really have never been to cities much. Coming to school here was a major step for me! I am having to learn to be streetwise.

"I was brought up in a very strict, religious home. It seemed to me that I got into trouble for almost everything I liked to do. Also, there were no other kids my age to play with at the school I attended. It was a very small church school, and I was very sheltered.

"As I got older, I got tired of not being able to do this or that on Saturday, and being punished if I did something that was not approved behavior. For example, I wasn't allowed to go swimming, play ball, throw a Frisbee, or any kind of sport on the Sabbath. I wasn't allowed to go to movies or dance or go to town with my friends. I did have home chores that I didn't mind, like chopping wood for three wood fires every night after school during the winter months. But for me, there were just too many dos and don'ts.

After some time and reflection I felt I had done them wrong. I went home and made amends.

"My home situation had deteriorated by the time I finished high school. My friend Joe suggested we could come here to be in art school together. I was already planning something like that, so it seemed to be the best thing to do.

"After some time and reflection, I felt sorry for my mom and dad, as I hadn't contacted them for over a year. I felt I had done them wrong. I recently went home and made amends for my behavior."

Eric told Connie about Thanksgiving, and shared his mom's parting words. Then he said, "Before, all the restrictions made no sense. I now know that the Sabbath should be a celebration of life; of God's creation. It should be treated as a fun time; not frivolous but the most fun of the whole week! In my estimation, my parents meant well but took things to an extreme."

Connie had been listening intently. She moved closer to Eric on the couch and put her hand on his arm. "Yes," she said, "I can see why you would dislike many of the things that were required of you. But in reality, the way you were brought up makes you stand out as a good and generous person who really cares about people."

For some time, they both just stared into the fire, deep in thought. After a while, Connie spoke again.

"You know, Eric, you were very lucky to have parents who loved you, even if they were very strict. They taught you the basics: love your neighbor as yourself, and love God ... the Bible's two greatest commandments."

Eric looked at her in surprise. "Sounds like you've been reading Scripture," he said.

Connie smiled at him. "Yeah, I decided to join the group with Johnny. We have been studying the Bible together with the Adventist pastor. For the first time in many years, I have found peace." She paused. "Yeah, that's it," she said. "I have found peace."

Eric thought to himself, *Can you beat that?*

After a few minutes, Connie said, "Eric, this has been a nice evening. I want to thank you for being my guest. If it's possible, maybe I could come to your place sometime? We could have lunch or something. I'd really like to see some more of your artwork."

Eric responded, "Sure, that would be fine."

Connie said, "I have an early-morning job interview, so I must go to bed now. You're welcome to stay over. I can pull out the couch, and I have extra sheets."

Eric hastily said he also had an early-morning appointment, so he needed to go back to his hotel to get some sleep.

She nodded. "Okay then; until we meet again." She squeezed his hand and unlocked the outside door.

Eric walked out into the night air. He was about five blocks from his hotel, so he walked briskly. When he came to a street that led to the docks and Third Street, he turned down it. He was deep in thought when, halfway down the street, he noticed a car parked on the side where he was walking. As he passed it, he could smell cigarette smoke.

His intuition told him he should change sides of the street. He walked across and picked up his pace. He had about two blocks to go. Without turning around, he started to jog. His goal was to reach the next block, where there were more lights.

That was when he heard the car start up and the screech of rubber on cobblestones. He began to run. He heard more screeching and realized the speeding car had jumped the curb. It was too late to do anything but dive into a hedge row close to a brick wall.

A few feet ahead of Eric, the car flattened the hedge and slammed into the building. The car pulled away and squealed around the next corner. He could hear the V8 engine roaring as it disappeared.

Eric had had the wind knocked out of him, and he rebruised his knees and elbows. His knees always seemed to be getting bruised. What had started out as a quiet, peaceful evening with a friend had become a nightmare! Why was this happening to him? Real fear overtook him.

Eric walked as fast as he could to the hotel, which was one block away. He reached it without further mishap and quickly went inside. There were only two people in the lobby. The lady in the white mink coat was arguing with the little man with the red face. Their conversation was quite animated.

Eric didn't go by the office but went straight to his room. He looked in the mirror. His face was scratched, and there was blood oozing from a cut over his left eye. His pants were in reasonable shape but were muddy at the knees. The rest of his clothes and shirt were dirt-streaked.

He noticed that his bathroom window was covered with plastic, finally. As tired as he was, he took a shower. Though it was quite cold in the room, the shower made up for it and felt good. He quickly changed into long johns, gave a prayer of thanksgiving for his life, and got into bed. His guardian angel had protected him, just like Psalm 91:11 said!

The chandelier shook back and forth over his head, as it did almost every night. He heard the sound of creaking bedsprings. As Eric fell into a deep sleep, he thought that it was good to have things back to normal ... even that.

CHAPTER 16

Fishing of a Sort

When he woke up, he decided to go to the docks and draw. Eric liked to hang around the old fishermen who sat mending nets. These were the grandfathers and fathers of those who now did the actual fishing. It was a rough way to make a living.

Over time, he had gotten to know several members of the older generation quite well. One of these old sea captains was Ned Faraday. Over time, the two of them became good friends. Ned seemed to enjoy being drawn, and Eric enjoyed the process.

That day, while Eric was drawing his friend, Ned told him a funny story about an art student named Ryan, who had come down to the docks to draw this beautiful old Maine dory that was tied up at the dock.

Ryan had asked Ned who owned it, and Ned said that he did.
Ryan then asked, "Would you sell this boat to me?"
Ned made it look like he was torn … should he sell his boat or not?
Ryan said, "I'll give you $40 for it."

After deliberating for some time, Ned finally agreed.

Ryan looked very pleased with himself, and they shook hands on the deal. Before Ryan left, he asked Ned to look after it until he returned the next day.

Ned said, "Sure will."

The next day Ryan returned to take his girlfriend out for a ride. Old Ned was there as they drew closer to the dock, but the boat wasn't. Ryan went all the way down the dock, looking between the fishing boats, but no dory was to be found. He walked back to Ned.

He asked, "Where is my boat?"

Old Ned responded, "I don't know. I haven't seen it since yesterday. Someone must have stolen it."

"Well, how am I to find it?" asked Ryan, concerned.

Ned shook his head. "I don't know. Sometimes they get 'borrowed,' but eventually, they show up."

"Well, it doesn't look like we get a boat ride today," Ryan said. He made a few other choice comments and disappeared down the wharf in a huff.

Ned concluded by telling Eric, with a sly smile, "I've sold that boat to art students many times over the years. My son just moves it to another dock for a week or so, where he sells it to another student, if possible. The funny thing is, it's not our boat. In fact, none of the fishermen here know whose boat it is. It's just always been here."

Eric stopped drawing for a moment. Even though it was very wrong, it was funny. He had to laugh along with Ned.

That day, due to the cold, Eric didn't stay at the dock too long. He put the finishing touches on his last sketch, showed it to Ned, then stowed his supplies and bid his friend farewell and Merry Christmas.

CHAPTER 17

Impressions of Junior Year

Christmas came and went, and before he knew it Eric was halfway through his third year of school. The competition in school was fierce but also, for the most part, friendly. By the time the second semester started, Eric, Johnny, and another art student were at the top of the class. Eric was starting to show his work, and people were beginning to buy his small sculptures and paintings. He felt a surge of accomplishment from this, and kept working hard to be the best that he could be.

In that time, his and Connie's relationship blossomed as well. She modeled three mornings a week for four-hour stints, but she always waited after a session so that they could eat together. Eric looked forward to this time with her. He could be himself, and apparently she liked who he was. She actually seemed to lock up to him, but she was not patronizing about it.

His relationship with Bobbie had also grown in a positive way; at least, he hoped that was the case. It seemed that as soon as she saw him on the street, she would start quieting down. Sometimes, when he walked by, she would still call out with the same crude phrases, but most of the time, she just stared at him. Lately, she had even started to wave (and then give him the finger). He could tell that Luce had noticed the same thing but had not connected the dots. She would yell, "Hey, you old bat out of hell, did you get stung by a bee?" Bobbie would only say, "Oh, shut up," or something similar.

Finally, he continued to escort Monique home from school on Mrs. Romano's behalf. Thankfully, they had no further run-ins. Nevertheless, Mrs. Romano told him one evening that she had decided to send her daughter away to get her out of that very difficult environment for a while. Monique would spend the summer with an aunt, then go to a different school for the fall semester, away from the city.

And just like that, the spring semester ended. Eric said his goodbyes to the Romanos, then to Connie. Connie would work in the city all summer, but Eric was going away to work with his uncle, who kept bees. Their goodbye was very sweet!

CHAPTER 18

Beware the Tides

Over the summer, the fear that had engulfed Eric after almost being run over (on purpose) shifted to the back of his mind. And that fall, as he started his fourth year, he still didn't have reason to think much about it, now that he no longer had a duty to protect Monique. In short, Eric's life seemed to be under less stress. He was able to focus on school for a change!

One clear fall day, Danny, another one of the painting students and someone who was from the area, suggested that he and Eric do some "plain-air" painting along the coast north of the city. Many artists went to this location to paint the rugged seacoast. Eric thought, with excitement and anticipation, that this would be a great opportunity. It took about two hours of driving. All along the route, the coast was dotted with lobster shacks, colorful lobster buoys, and fishing boats anchored in beautiful island-protected bays.

He and Danny talked the whole way about the painting teacher and his skillful use of white paper for highlights. They agreed he was a master watercolor painter and had the respect of the student body. He was also a kind man and a very good teacher. Eric said he enjoyed his classes and studied his works because they were so fresh in appearance; they were some of the most beautiful works of art that he had ever seen.

They reached their destination. The lighthouse was a short distance away. Beyond, waves crashed onto the granite rocks. They were running high, about two feet, and the tide was almost all the way out, so there were a lot of tidepools and interesting rock formations visible.

"This is a perfect setting for a seascape," Eric said. They set their easels up halfway down a granite rock face in the shelter of a rock outcropping where they could see the lighthouse, then they began to paint.

Time slipped by quickly, and the waves began to slam against the rocks closer to them. Eric knew he would not be able to finish the painting at that location. As usual, they would take the canvases back to class and finish at the art school.

Danny had set up about fifty feet away, a little closer to the incoming tide. Eric yelled, "Hey, looks like the tide is pushing in."

Danny replied, "Yeah, give me another ten minutes."

"Okay," called Eric.

> Danny looked up and yelled back at Eric, "Run, run! Rogue wave!"

Eric looked out to sea again. The sun was behind a cloud, and the wind had picked up. Then he turned back to the painting on his easel. He sensed that something was different. He quickly turned and looked again at the horizon. There had been some islands ... small outcroppings of land in the distance ... the islands were gone! The horizon was gone! He looked upward and saw the horizon line up against the clouds. Eric yelled to Danny.

Danny looked up and yelled back at Eric, "Run, run! Rogue wave!"

Eric's easel and open tacklebox were out of reach. He grabbed his canvas and a handful of brushes and started running up the rock face. He and Danny were both about twenty yards from safety when the wave broke. The incoming surge caught Eric about knee-high and continued moving almost to the parking lot.

Danny was caught waist-high. He lost his footing as the surge took him up the hill. It tried to take him with it as it receded; however, he was able to grab onto a rock with one arm while holding onto his canvas with the other. Danny got up and sat at the edge of the parking lot, soaked.

Eric and Danny looked at each other as the surf returned to normal.

"Well, so much for my easel! I just bought it not too long ago." Danny said.

Eric responded, "At least you had sense enough to put your tackle box up here. Mine is somewhere down there in the surf."

"Well," Danny said, "We are both alive. These waves show up a couple of times a year and usually take their toll."

As they drove back to school, Eric and Danny didn't talk much. Danny let Eric off at the school, then drove away to where he lived across town. Eric realized that God had saved his life again, as well as Danny's. If Danny hadn't been there with him, he would not have seen the danger he was in … and vice versa! Alone, either one of them very likely would have either drowned or been seriously hurt, but by God's grace they had been spared together.

He was starting to think that his life seemed to be always on the edge. And he also saw that the God he had put in the background had stayed with him despite that. *My life must change*, he thought. *I'm just not going to last if I don't wise up.*

CHAPTER 19

Peer Critique

Danny and Eric became best friends after the big wave incident and would have several more adventures together. Eric was invited to Danny's house on several occasions to stay overnight, especially on the days they went sailing. Thus Eric got to know Danny's mother, father, sister, and brothers, too.

He learned that Danny's mom was a devout Catholic, and his sister had followed in her footsteps. Danny's dad didn't appear to believe in any church; however, he was a very kind gentleman. Eric knew that Danny had joined Johnny's church group and was regularly attending church. Yet when Danny had been baptized into the Adventist church, his mom showed no signs of disagreement. She only said, "I just want you to be happy."

When Eric saw how well they all got along, one day his curiosity got the best of him. He asked Danny why he had left a nice Catholic family tradition to join a church that Eric thought was so legalistic. In Eric's mind, he told Danny, the church he had belonged to could not see the forest for the trees. He said, "It seems like a big change from Sunday to Saturday worship. I mean, why would you do that?"

Danny answered, "Eric, there were too many things that just didn't make sense. For example, I couldn't make sense out of being stuck in purgatory after dying until some relative got on the ball and paid a bunch of money so I could have forgiveness.

"The Bible says in numerous places that we who die are asleep. And when Jesus comes back, He wakes us up. We will then get the reward we deserve; those who make a commitment to Him while alive are raised up to meet Him in the clouds and will be changed in the twinkling of an eye.

"The idea of indulgences was also foreign to me. The loving Savior that I have come to know would not be any part of this. I can't pay or work my way to Heaven. The Bible says that eternal life is a gift." Danny continued, "Eric, the idea of going and confessing to a man that I know personally, who has as many or more faults in his life than I do, just isn't right. The Bible says that Christ is the only One who can forgive sin. But the worst lie that is being taught by the church is that when they take communion, the wafer and the wine are Christ's real body."

> Danny said, "Worshiping Christ through simple prayer has given me a peace that I have no words to express."

Danny paused. "Eric, you said that you quit your church because they were too legalistic. That may be true of some, but not all. I was brought up a Catholic, but since I have gotten to know Johnny and you and the group, I have learned the simplicity of worship. Worshiping Christ through simple prayer, knowing that I am speaking directly to my Father in heaven, has given me a peace of mind and heart that, in all honesty, I have no words to express.

"And Pastor Ken has been so different from anyone I have ever met. We openly share experiences, but he has never mentioned anything that we are doing wrong. I don't think he even notices or thinks that way. In fact, he will tell us where he has fallen short when he feels like he has hurt someone else. It amazes us how truly humble he is.

"He just talks about the love of Jesus as it relates to His death on the cross. He says, 'Just keep your eyes on how Jesus shared His Father's love with people.' Always seeing the faults in others simply means that you need to see how Jesus dealt with people. He was trying to teach the people, not point fingers at their faults. Pastor Ken says there is plenty of bad in the world, but we should focus on the two great commandments."

Danny concluded, "All of us in Johnny's group see Pastor Ken's spirit of peace and love for each of us. We talk about him a lot. He knows all of us by name. He has been such a good friend."

Wow, Eric thought, *I've never met an Adventist pastor like Pastor Ken. Where in the world did he come from?* For weeks, he thought about what Danny had said.

CHAPTER 20

Monique Returns

One day after school, Eric stopped by the sandwich shop. It was almost 7:00 p.m. The place had its usual group of art students at the tables, but there were several vacant tables as it was past the supper hour. Eric decided to relax before ordering. He chose a table near the front window and sat with his back to the wall and his pack beside him.

The remaining supper clients started to leave, and as the place cleared out, he could better see the counter area. Mrs. Romano was working the register with her usual efficiency, smiling pleasantly at each customer. He caught her eye, and she nodded briefly. Then Johnny came in with a new girl from school, but they didn't see Eric. They sat in a back corner, out of the bright lights. Eric had seen a few of the girl's photos hanging in the photo studio. She was quite good! He was glad to see Johnny with someone; Johnny had some health issues and was sick quite often.

He turned his attention to the window. Like many artists before him, Eric was fascinated with street scenes. The streetwalkers were out en masse. Two big, black sedans were parked across the street. And a navy ship must have just come in because there were many sailors mixed in with the crowd. He had a literal window into life on the street.

He was so intent on the action that he was unaware that someone had come up behind him. A soft voice brought him back to reality. He looked up and was shocked to see Monique standing there.

She said, "Would you like something to eat?"

"Wow," he said, "You look so grown up. I hardly recognized you!"

She laughed easily. "Well, I'm really glad you noticed."

Eric stopped staring. They hadn't seen one another for months, and he could see that Monique was no longer a kid. She had grown up into a beautiful young woman. He realized that he was glad to see her, but he felt almost guilty. He thought to himself, *Is it because I have developed feelings for Connie?*

He put these thoughts aside. "I would like a bowl of tomato soup and a grilled cheese sandwich," he said.

Monique smiled. "I'll be right back," she said.

Eric was still in thought when she set the tray in front of him.

"Are you going to ask me to join you?" Monique asked.

"Of course," Eric answered. "I'm just so surprised. I thought you were going to be gone this school year. I'd like to have you join me. I apologize for being so slow."

She sat down across from him, smiling.

Eric asked, "Could you tell me where you have been and about your travels?"

"Sure," she said. Monique talked quietly for a long time, filling him in on her time away. Then she said, "It's important that you understand why my mom wanted me to leave.

"My mom is convinced that the company wants our store. We are one of only three buildings on this street that they don't own or control. After my father's death and what my uncle went through, they apparently thought we would have had enough and leave. That they would offer to pay a small price for the store—nothing near its worth—and we would be out. But my mother didn't want to sell out, because the store was left to her by her great-grandparents, who started the business in the 1920s.

"She has been so worried that they would kidnap and abuse me! Then there was the incident on the street when you saved us from getting hit by the truck. And they even tried to run you down. So she sent me away.

"But no one has come to bother us since, so she thought it was all right for me to come back now. I'm going to work with her in the shop and do home study this semester. I'll finish my senior year at the high school in the spring. That's about it."

Eric said, "I'm glad to see you back, safe and sound."

Monique got up, smiling. "It's good to see you, too, Eric," she said. She walked back to the counter and conversed with her mother for a few moments, then went through the curtains. Eric put a tip on the table, put on his backpack, and left the shop.

CHAPTER 21

An Evening with Connie

It had started to snow. The cold air was brisk and felt good! He decided to go back to school for a while and draw. That evening, Connie was modeling for a senior drawing class. He would walk her home after class if he could.

He bounded up the steps and past the security guard, Mr. Thompson. He was an older, good-natured gentleman. He talked with a lisp, so students always made fun of him behind his back. Interestingly, he knew they did it but wasn't upset. He just played it up a bit, and everyone would have a great laugh. Eric was drawn to Mr. Thompson because he really looked after the students' work. And Eric knew that Mr. Thompson liked him because, when Eric was painting late in the evening, he always sat by Eric's easel, talking and joking about many things. They laughed a lot, which proved to be good therapy for Eric.

Inside, Eric looked through the window in the door where Connie was working. She was doing a seated pose. He went down the hall to the drawing studio to work on a small drawing for about an hour. Then he went back to see if Connie was ready to go. The class had finished, and she was just leaving through the front doors. From the top of the stairs, he called to her.

She turned. "There you are," Connie said. "I was wondering if you were anywhere around. Would you like to get a bite to eat? I'm starved."

"Yes," Eric said. "I've already eaten at Romano's, but I could eat a little dessert."

"Sounds good to me," she said.

They walked a couple of blocks and ended up in front of Carmin's Bar & Grill. "The food is good," Connie said, "and the prices are very reasonable."

They entered and sat down at the counter. The waitress knew Eric, so they exchanged greetings. Then she looked at Connie. "I know you, too," she said. "You're one of our models." Connie nodded. The waitress took their orders and left.

Eric and Connie started to converse. The food arrived and they began to eat. He told her what Monique had said.

"Well, I feel so sorry for those people!" Connie said. "Besides being your friends, they are such a positive influence in the neighborhood."

Eric said that Mrs. Romano hadn't been bothered for at least eight months, so she was breathing a little easier.

"I'm still worried," Connie said as she finished her supper.

They ordered apple pie with ice cream for dessert. Afterward, Connie asked, "Would you like to come over tonight to study the Bible with me? I'm still going through The Sermon on the Mount."

Eric said, "Sounds like a plan!"

When they reached her apartment, Eric waited in the living room while Connie went to change out of her street clothes. She came back dressed in a long, pink nightgown and barefoot. She sat on the sofa by Eric with her feet curled up under her. They pondered the text, "The meek shall inherit the earth" from Psalm 37.

They talked at length about what it meant to be meek. What the world taught was that if you didn't take it, it would be taken from you. If you wanted to get ahead, you would very likely have to push someone else out of the way. Sure, help someone; because if you do, they are possibly going to help you. But if you're not going to get something out of it, don't waste your time.

Eric and Connie surmised that meekness had a lot to do with unselfishness, and that Christ honored those who were meek and of low status because, for the most part, they couldn't help themselves.

It had gotten really late, and Eric was starting to fall asleep. Connie said, "I'll get you a blanket. You can stay and sleep on the sofa." He started to object, but he didn't have the energy to resist. He was asleep before she returned.

The smell of coffee awoke him. He wasn't on the sofa anymore; he was on the carpeted floor! He must have rolled off during the night. Since Eric was already dressed, he got up and walked into the bathroom. He splashed water on his face. It had the desired effect; he was now wide awake. Eric combed his hair and walked into the kitchen. Connie had already set the food on the table.

She asked, "Well, how was the floor?"

He smiled, "I didn't know the difference." Then Eric observed that he was going to be late to school again!

She said, "Well, we had better eat and get going."

He prayed for the food, and they ate. Then they prayed for the day and walked to the corner. "Thanks for the good breakfast," he said. "See you in class tomorrow."

"Ok, see ya," Connie said, and they went their separate ways.

CHAPTER 22

Broken Figures

Eric ducked into his sculpture class. Tomorrow the teacher would be there for critique, and the figure he was working on had cracked. It was made from alabaster, so he mixed stone dust with resin, filled in the crack, and left it to harden. A while later he sanded it, since he needed to make it look like the rest of the sculpture as much as possible. It was going to take a lot of sanding! The noon hour came and he shifted gears, working through the afternoon in his painting class. Eric left school at 6:00 p.m. and went to Romano's to eat supper.

The usual patrons were there, but the atmosphere was subdued and very quiet. People were not gesturing and talking like the normal crowd. Johnny and his photographer friend, Shelly, were sitting in the center of the room. They motioned for him to join them.

"Hey, Eric, I haven't seen you for a long time. What gives?" Johnny said.

Before Eric could say anything, Shelly spoke up, "We heard that you were spending a lot of time with Connie lately."

Johnny added, "That's not a bad thing, but you did sort of drop off the map." He smiled at Eric good-naturedly. "Anyway," he said, "how about some food?"

Eric said, "Yes, that sounds good. I'll put in my order."

Then Johnny said, "The old man who used to work here was killed yesterday evening while crossing High Street, about three blocks from here. Monique and her mom are pretty broken up about it. Mrs. Romano is not here, but Monique and a friend of the family are minding the store."

Eric was shocked. Was it Uncle Dalio? He needed to talk to Monique. He left the conversation hanging and headed toward the counter. All of a sudden, he heard a door slam shut behind him. As he turned, he was hit from the side and knocked down. Fortunately, he landed on the floor between two tables. The other guests seemed shocked. He heard more cursing and noise as a large person pushed through the line. Another customer stumbled, barely missing a table and landing against the counter.

The big, rude man was gesturing and talking loudly to the older woman behind the counter. "Where's Romano?" he asked in a surly tone.

"She is not here; she has—"

He talked over her roughly, "Well, tell her we need to talk. She knows who I am. Where is my sandwich? It should have been done an hour ago!"

> The old man who used to work here was killed yesterday evening while crossing High Street.

The older lady spoke again, "Could you please tell me your name? Then I can—"

"This will do," he said as he grabbed the sandwich that was just being rung up for a customer. He turned around, and people dove out of his way. He left as quickly as he had come, slamming the door again.

Eric was beginning to get the picture. He had seen this man several times in the entryway to the apartments where Luce and Bobbie worked, and he was the same one who had beat up the girl on the street. There was something sinister about him. He seemed able to get away with almost anything he did. Whoever was behind him was very powerful, indeed!

The sandwich shop regained some semblance of order. Johnny and Shelly asked Eric if he was okay. "Wow, that guy was crazy!" Johnny commented. Then he said, "We are late for class. We'll see you later."

Eric still needed supper, so he again approached the counter. Monique appeared through the curtained door. He could see that she had been crying.

She said quietly, "Eric, it's so good to see you. What would you like to eat?"

He said, "I'll take the usual: tomato soup and a grilled cheese sandwich."

"Alright," she said, "It will be just a minute. I'll bring it to your table, and then we can talk."

"That will be good," Eric said and went to a table away from the main foot traffic.

A few minutes later, Monique was there with the food. She sat down across from him. He was always surprised by her beauty; even now, when she had dark circles around her eyes. He said a prayer for the food and started to eat his supper. Then Monique began to speak.

"Eric, yesterday was terrible! Uncle Dalio went to visit his old friend on Mott Street. He was crossing High Street when a car ran a red light in broad daylight, ran him over, and kept right on going! He was pronounced dead on the scene. My mom is with his body at the funeral home, making arrangements for a spring burial.

"On top of this, Mom has a friend with connections to the company who gave her a heads-up on some things. Mom wanted me to tell you that one of them has to do with you, Eric. Apparently, your being in the shadows and drawing the house across the street has come to their attention. They don't like someone closely observing their business. If you keep it up, they will give you a hard lesson!"

A cold chill went through Eric as he listened. Monique was looking at him worriedly.

"That's not all," she said. "They think Bobbie has been leading you on, so they punished her. I guess the big guy beat her up badly. Mom's friend said one of Bobbie's eyes is blackened and shut and she has other cuts and bruises. She has not been out and about her business."

Eric was shocked. He had had no idea that sketching someone would lead to so much trouble! Bobbie being hurt because of him was a terrible turn of events.

Monique continued, "My mother and I are both so worried about you! They know who you are. You need to be on the lookout. In fact, we think you should go away for a while, like I did."

How some people could have the power of life and death over others in such a negative way was a great concern. Eric would have to figure this out. Monique waited while her words sank in. Finally, Eric spoke.

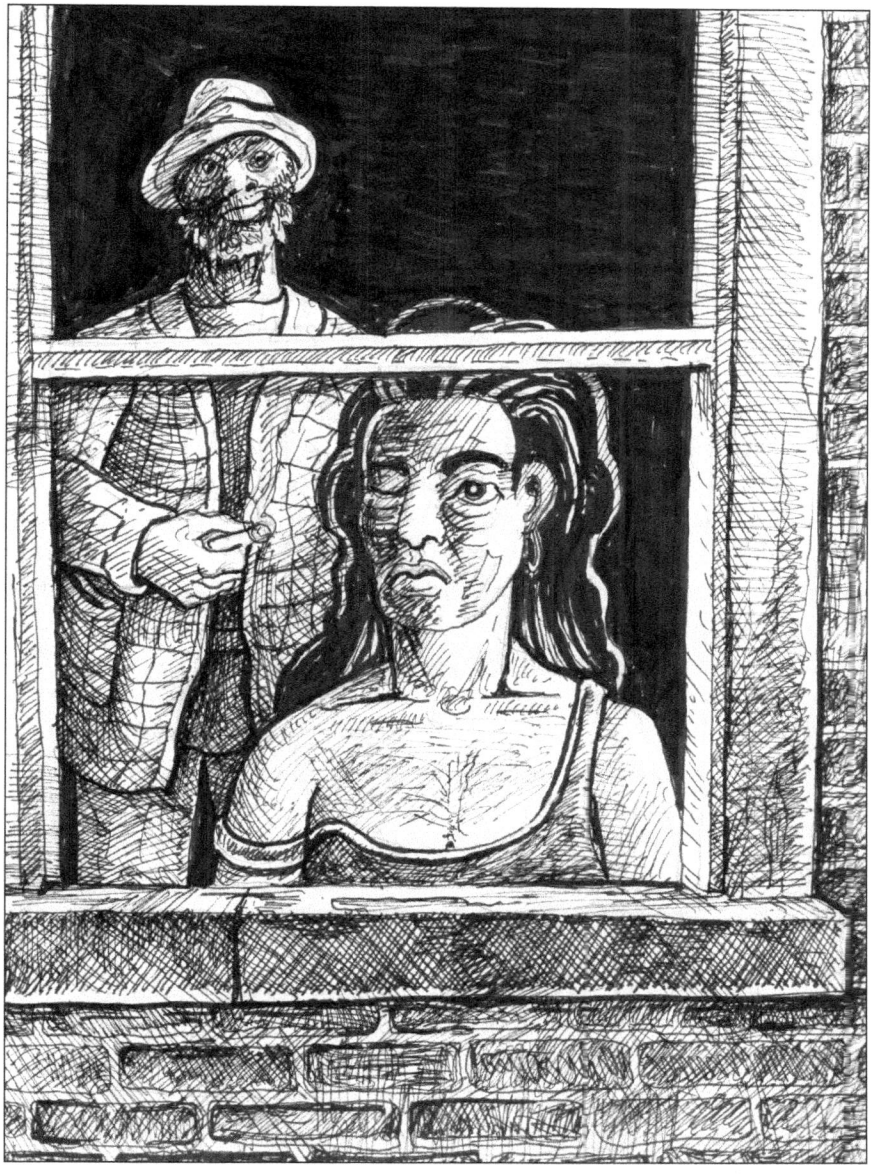

"Monique, first of all, I need to finish this semester of school. There is less than a month left. Second, it's true that I'm afraid to be seen on Third Street for fear they will hurt Bobbie more, but she sort of depends on me to go by each day to make her feel better ... just seeing someone who cares for her, even from a distance."

Monique smiled for the first time since the beginning of the conversation. "You could get a disguise like I did when you used to walk me home."

"Yeah, maybe that would work," Eric said, "Or I could just wait till a big crowd goes by. Regardless, this means I won't be able to sketch Bobbie anymore." Eric felt very paranoid at that moment. Then he made a decision. "Let's pray," he said.

He and Monique bowed their heads. Monique put her hand in his as if to gain some of his strength. Eric asked God to strengthen Monique and Mrs. Romano. He asked that God help them to take heart that the Holy Spirit was there and that He would keep them safe. He also prayed for their reunion with Uncle Dalio, who had been a good and kind man. He asked that they would see him again when Jesus came back to the world to take those who loved Him to Heaven. Finally, Eric asked God to help Monique and Mrs. Romano to see that He was there for them.

His voice broke as he finished. Eric dropped his hands to his sides and kept his head bowed. He felt embarrassed because of his emotions.

"I'm not used to prayers like that," Monique said. She got up, then said, "My mother wanted you to have this address and telephone number. This is a lawyer that we have used for troubles in the past. She called him, so he is waiting to talk to you. Please see him, Eric."

Eric thanked her for the information.

Monique said, "I need to get back to the counter. I'll see you later."

What was left of Eric's supper was cold, but he ate it anyway. Before he stepped outside, he put the hood of his jacket over his head. The night air was invigorating, as usual. He walked quickly toward his building. As he passed Bobbie's, he saw her gesturing in her window. He could see what Monique was talking about. Something about her face didn't look right, but it was hard to make out from this distance.

Even through his minor disguise, Bobbie seemed to figure out who he was, as she made a barely perceptible gesture with her head. Eric felt

like they were having positive communication. Still, he walked quickly toward his building and immediately went up to his room.

The next day, Eric decided to eat lunch at Romano's. With his hood over his head, he made his way down Third Street and walked into the shop. No one was behind the counter when he sat down at a table by the window. Then he saw the large, black sedan parked in front of the shop. He could see from the exhaust that the car was running. *What are they doing here?* he immediately asked himself.

He noticed a commotion behind the counter. Two men appeared through the hanging curtain. Eric still had his hood up, so after looking around at the patrons, the men just walked out, slamming the door as they went.

As soon as they left, Eric ran quickly behind the counter and through the curtain. Monique and her mom were sitting on the floor, crying and holding each other. The small table and two chairs he and Monique had sat in over a year ago were tipped over, and food was scattered on the floor.

"What happened?" he asked. He took Mrs. Romano by the hand, helping her to her feet. This woman who had always seemed so strong and capable now seemed so frail! He felt her hand grip his, her strength slowly returning as he righted the chairs and helped her sit in one. Then Eric went to Monique, who was already trying to stand. She gave him a weak smile while he helped her to the other chair.

Mrs. Romano finally spoke. "Eric, could you please tell the other guests that tonight's meal is on the house, and put the *Closed* sign up in the window?"

He immediately did as she had asked. When he came back into the back room, he asked, "Where is your other helper?"

"She left earlier, so she wasn't here. Thank God," she replied.

Eric asked, "Did they hurt you?"

"Not badly. They just pushed us to the floor and shouted at us." Then she explained, "They told us to comply with the boss's orders or else. 'If you don't,' they said, 'We'll have a little surprise for you.' One of them held up his cigarette lighter, flicking it on and off a couple of times. He said, 'You get my drift?' Then they left."

Eric's mind was racing. He knew these men weren't kidding, and it seemed like law enforcement was looking the other way. He could walk away from all of this. It really wasn't any of his business ... but he couldn't do that ... these were God's children and his good friends!

He faced the two women and solemnly said, "I don't know how this is going to turn out, but something's got to give. To me, you are both like family! With God's help, I will come up with something to get us through all of this." Then he prayed for their safety and for God to send His Spirit of protection.

Mrs. Romano walked him to the door and locked the entrance as he left. Once again, as he went by Bobbie's window, their eyes met for just a moment. He hurriedly kept walking.

CHAPTER 23

A Civil Consultation and a Jarring Awakening

Eric confided in Connie everything that had been going on. She, too, urged him to leave the city, but he would not. He felt responsible for Bobbie and the Romanos. At 1:30 on an afternoon not long after praying with the Romanos, Eric took a cab across town to see the lawyer.

He arrived at an imposing building about two miles from the art school. He had a note of introduction from Mrs. Romano and a list of events he had compiled with dates and the names of the streets where they had taken place.

The building was a newer structure. The carpet was thick and rich-looking, with wall tapestries to match. Gilt chandeliers hung from the ceiling. The overall feeling of the place was old, established wealth. The lawyer's office was on the second floor. Eric knocked on the door, and a voice said, "Come in."

The secretary was by the window watering some plants. She was middle-aged with vestiges of good looks from years past. She gave Eric a genuine smile and motioned him to a chair. "You're Eric," she said with assurance. "Well, you're right on time. As soon as Mr. Goldman gets off the phone, he will see you. It shouldn't be long."

The secretary started busying herself about the desk. Soon she said, "You can see him now."

Eric entered a room with a large wooden desk. Behind it sat Mr. Goldman, a middle-aged man with heavy jowls.

He said, "Good afternoon, Eric."

Eric responded, "Good afternoon, sir."

Mr. Goldman said, "Please have a seat."

Eric sat in a soft chair with a straight back. Though it felt comfortable, he was a bit uneasy. Mr. Goldman, however, seemed friendly enough, and spoke first.

"Mrs. Romano called and said you were going to visit. She told me a little about what you wanted to know."

Eric nodded.

Mr. Goldman looked steadily at Eric and said, "Before you begin, let me tell you what you are dealing with.

"'The company,' as I call it, has been in that part of the city for a long time. Years ago, they were small. They were a group of off-color business associates who dealt in illegal liquor sales and some prostitution. The illegal liquor required money laundering and some strong-arm tactics. Over time, they got into hard drugs and territorial battles with similar organizations. As time passed, murders were committed.

"At first, most of what went on was among people involved in their business. In later years, collateral damage became more prevalent. The city began to feel the strain that the company was causing businesses and the community. Their drug dealers were getting school kids hooked. Prostitution became more and more open. Law enforcement officers switched allegiance and began protecting certain groups.

"Today the city is working to rid local government of those who are paid to look the other way. The process is long, but it is slowly beginning to work.

"Eric, you have seen quite a bit of what happens on Third Street. And from what Mrs. Romano says, you have come under scrutiny from the company. As God knows, this isn't a good thing. Right now there is very little anyone can do to protect you—or any other citizen—if the company decides to hurt you." Mr. Golden paused and cleared his throat. "I've said a lot for the purpose of background. Now, what can I do for you?"

Eric sat quietly for a few moments. Then he said, "Is there anything that can be done for the Romanos? I have tried to help as much as I can, but now I fear I may be more of a liability to them."

Mr. Goldman said, "I believe as Marisa does that it's probably best for you to leave the city as soon as you can. I understand that you are at the art school and will finish shortly. Good. After that, get away for a while and let things simmer down."

Eric said, "Yes, but what will happen to the Romanos?"

Mr. Goldman sat back in his chair and thought for a short while. Then he said, "I think eventually things will get better, as more pressure is put on the company by local law enforcement and state authorities. At least we can hope and pray that things will reach an equilibrium."

Eric opened his mouth to speak but Mr. Goldman continued, "Your concern for the Romanos is admirable, and I like your courage, but what's going on here is bigger than you can handle. Eric, please understand that until something changes, you could be in great danger. That bunch never forgets to cover their tracks. If they think you saw something, they will make sure you never see anything else again.

> Eric, please understand that until something changes, you could be in great danger.

"If I were you, I wouldn't walk down that street any more for a while. Try to stay in groups of students when you go out. Don't get caught alone on the street, especially at night. Be on your guard constantly."

Mr. Goldman looked up at the clock. "It's time for my next appointment," he said. He stood up, walked around the desk, and put out his hand.

Eric shook it. "Thank you for your time," he said.

As they walked to the door, Mr. Goldman smiled. "I wish you good luck," he said.

Eric went down the stairs and out the front door. He stepped into a phone booth and called a cab. It was only a couple of minutes before a yellow cab pulled up to the curb. Eric got in the back and gave the driver the location of the art school.

They pulled away from the curb. The driver was a pleasant older man who must have been driving in the city for many years. He began to tell Eric about some of the changes on the streets around the art school. Eric enjoyed the conversation and learned quite a bit of history.

Suddenly, the driver stopped talking. Then he said, "Somebody is following us. Did you know that someone was back there?"

"No." Eric felt a huge rush of adrenalin. "Is there any way we can lose them?"

"Yeah," the driver said. At the next intersection, he drove through a yellow light, took a left around the corner, and then took another turn to the right.

Up ahead, Eric could see a red light and a stopped car. There was also a school bus parked on his left. Its motor compartment was open, and it looked as if repairs were being done. As they approached the intersection, they slowed. Cars crossed through before them, heading toward the city.

"I think we've lost them," Eric said to the driver. Just as the words left his mouth, he heard screeching tires. Eric looked back and saw a black sedan speeding toward them. The taxi driver shouted, "They're going to hit us! Get out."

Eric already had his door partly open, but it was too late. The sedan rammed into the back of the taxi, pushing it forward into the intersection. Eric's unlatched door flew open upon impact, and he was thrown out of the vehicle. He landed under the bus behind its front wheels, just as the taxi was hit by the crossing traffic.

He heard screeching brakes and tires and loud crashes. He got a glimpse out of the corner of his eye of the black sedan pulling back from the intersection, backing down a side street, then turning and slowly driving off. At that instant, Eric lost consciousness.

He awoke against the curb, still under the bus. Eric could see feet running past. A crowd was gathering. He felt like he was in some sort of dream state. Everything was in slow motion. He heard police sirens, and the large crowd was yelling something.

To his complete surprise, he seemed relatively unscathed. His left shoulder hurt, and he could barely move it. His right arm was sore but usable (apparently, it was not broken). His right knee was cut and bleeding, and he could put no weight on it, and there was blood on the sleeve of his jacket. But all things considered …. He tried crawling and found that he could. He moved toward the back of the bus.

Everyone was looking toward the intersection. He stood up behind the bus, dusted himself off as best as he could, and started to slowly walk the last ten blocks back to the hotel. The whole way, strangely enough, no one seemed to notice him. Everyone was running the other way.

As he walked, he half expected to be run down by the black sedan. He decided not to go in the front of the hotel. He reached the back alley, used the delivery entrance, and painfully climbed the stairs to the lobby. He looked carefully around the room before he entered. It was still only 3:00 in the afternoon, and the lobby was vacant. He walked slowly to the office.

Junior started to get his mail, but quickly turned around. "Eric, what in the world happened to you?"

Eric tried to speak but had no energy. He was very lightheaded and felt sick to his stomach. The Romanos and Mr. Goldman had been right. He had been totally naïve and unprepared for this turn of events.

Junior came from behind the desk and helped Eric sit down. He got him a cup of coffee. Then, slowly, Eric told him the whole story from beginning to end. As he talked, the radio played soft music.

While Eric was talking, Junior examined him. Eric had no broken bones or serious cuts or bruises. Junior bandaged Eric's knee and put some salve on a few facial cuts. In a very short time, he looked and felt much better. As Eric talked, Junior looked first shocked and then angry. He seemed to want to say something but remained quiet until Eric had finished. Then Junior took over the conversation.

"You have been very lucky, Eric. I have had to find a way to live with these organized criminals. This is my home, but it is not a good neighborhood any more. I have seen the streets change over the past few years, from addicting our kids, to drugs, to kidnapping and rape. The few people who remain clean, like the Romanos, have faced death brought on by this 'company.' Someone even approaches Mr. Jones every so often.

"Thus far, he has been 'left alone.' But I know of at least two other deaths because of people going up against them. You, Eric, are not going to survive very long here … between your close involvement with the Romano family and this business where they think you're spying on their prostitutes … it really has me worried. The saving grace is that you are leaving school after this semester. If I were you, I would not come back; at least not for a long time. I hope you use good judgment in this situation."

Eric said, "I was going to take summer classes, but now I've decided to leave after this semester and come back in another year."

The music was interrupted suddenly by a news bulletin. There was a report of a multicar accident on Main Street. Two people had been killed, one of whom was a taxi driver. The other was a woman who had been driving through the intersection with the green light. Two other people had been taken to the hospital for bruises and then would be released shortly to answer questions. There would be a police investigation because bystanders had seen the taxicab stopped at the red light, then struck from behind and pushed forward.

Eric and Junior looked at each other. Then Eric said, "Junior, thanks for everything and for being such a good friend." He got up stiffly and walked to his room.

Tomorrow was Saturday. This would give him a chance to rest and think of what to do. Eventually, he was going to have to start going to church. He had the strong impression that God was preserving his life for a reason.

CHAPTER 24

The Fruits of One's Labor

The weekend came. Friday night was the school's official, end-of-the-year party. Awards would be given out, and then everyone would be taken to a well-known seafood restaurant. Eric did not want to go. Connie could not go either; she had a degree in psychology from a university in a nearby city, and this was the week of her practicum. However, his teachers had told him not to miss it.

Eric received awards for best sculpture design and for his drawing of Bobbie. He felt really happy with his progress at art school, despite the 'extracurricular activity' in his life. Afterward, he and Johnny, along with some others, decided to skip the big dinner and instead go to Cremo's together. They arrived around 5:00. Shelly, the photographer, joined them in time to eat.

Halfway through dinner, Eric began to feel a little sick to his stomach. He had drunk a little wine, and he felt a little tipsy, but alcohol did not normally affect him like most people. He was able to shake it off at first and continued to talk to Johnny and the others. After they finished their meal, Johnny and Shelly went to the dance floor, but Eric was starting to feel quite sick. He excused himself from a conversation with some other students and left the restaurant. The cold air seemed to help clear his head.

As Eric turned on High Street, he sensed he was being followed. He joined a small group of sailors moving in the direction of Third, then glanced back and saw the nose of a black sedan at the corner he had just left. He was only two long and two short blocks from the hotel. He looked again and saw that the sedan had turned the corner, but fortunately the street was full of cars. Eric walked as quickly as he could to the Third Street intersection, crossed over High, and turned down Third. The sedan went straight by Third and kept going. Apparently, he had lost them.

When Eric stepped up onto the curb, he almost fell. He began weaving from side to side. His coordination was way off; his depth perception was non-existent. People began to look at him as if he were drunk or on drugs.

Eric reached out to touch the wall and managed to walk along the side of the buildings while bent partway over. As he went by Bobbie's, he was vaguely aware that she was there. After stumbling several times, he finally reached the hotel. He staggered up the stairs. He was now only able to see a blur. Somehow, he managed to get to his room and close the door. Then everything went black.

CHAPTER 25

The Samaritan and the Artist

Bobbie covered herself with a shawl. It had been a slow evening. In fact, the whole month had been a real stress for her. She felt trapped. She *was* trapped.

Her days were usually not so very complicated. She and Luce were always together. Bobbie slept from 5:00 in the morning to 3:00 in the afternoon and started work at about 4:00. As long as she and Luce followed the rules, they were left alone. They were warm in the winter, cool in the summer, and had three days a month off. She and Luce got a percentage from each client ... even if the reality was that they usually got a lot less than they were supposed to.

Then along came that art student. Bobbie's face had healed pretty well, but she still had to use a lot of makeup to cover her blackened eye. Her boss had been brutal, saying she was leading the boy on. She knew the truth: they were afraid of anyone closely watching their behavior, even if prostitution was only a small part of their business. They had said never to communicate with that student again.

Nevertheless, she did. It was Bobbie's way of getting back at them. And Eric—they'd only actually spoken that once, but she never forgot a name—seemed to be aware of the danger he was in, at least to some degree. Lately he wore that hood.

This evening was different, however. When he went by he seemed ... very drunk. He staggered as he crossed the street. He had never seemed like the drinking kind. This made Bobbie very uneasy. Her instincts told her that this was not good at all.

Bobbie really wished that she could be free from all of this. Getting out was a dream that she had been harboring for a long time.

Originally, she had come to the city as an uneducated fifteen-year-old girl to find herself. Looking for work to support herself, it had not taken her long to find the wrong kinds of friends and get caught in the sordid web of abuse, drugs, and then prostitution.

Why should I care so much about that boy? she said to herself. *Am I just getting soft in my old age?* No ... something told her that her interest in Eric came from somewhere else. She was old enough to know it was not "true love." She was just not used to someone getting close to her; especially someone who was just ... *there*, and hardly spoke. She could see that Eric was an honest person with a sweet spirit. She was drawn by his kindness and gentleness.

He also brought back her mothering instincts, which had long been suppressed. Bobbie had once had a son who was born from her profession; but he had been lost to drugs and to the men who had been her clients.

And now, she couldn't say why, she felt somehow responsible for Eric, and she cherished the feeling. *How did this happen?* She found it hard to sleep that night. Finally she drifted off, but when she woke the next day, the sense of uneasiness was still with her.

That evening, Eric did not go by; she was sure of it. She even told Luce to watch for him as well (with Luce warning her not ever to be caught communicating with him). Another day dawned, and Bobbie was getting super worried. Luce in turn became more worried about Bobbie, fearing she would do something stupid. Luce told Bobbie she knew her and could see where this was all going.

A second evening went by. The wondering and waiting for a glimpse of that strange, special boy were terrible for Bobbie. She did not want to eat or sleep. Eric was obviously very sick or worse.

Monday morning at 5:00 a.m., she decided to leave her post and go find him. She calculated that she could be back by 6:00 a.m. or sooner. The person in charge of her and Luce would not look in on them until much later. He would probably be sleeping off a hangover, anyway, so no one would be the wiser. Just in case, Luce would tell anyone who asked that Bobbie was very sick and had gone to the drugstore. Luce said she was very much against the plan, but she knew she could not stop Bobbie.

Bobbie knew the hotel would be locked. However, in the past, she had gone in through the back to reach clients. She felt confident that she could still get in via the old entrance to the laundry and delivery rooms where, in years gone by, block ice and milk had been delivered. At one time, a key had been left under a steel milk jug, then above the door. She searched for it, but it was no longer in either place. Then she simply tried the door, and to Bobbie's surprise it opened.

She stepped into the dimly lit hallway and felt her way along until she reached the bottom of the stairs leading to the hotel lobby. She quickly climbed the narrow stairs and peeked through the door. Daylight flooded the lobby, but there was not a soul around.

> Bobbie looked through the guest register for Eric's name, then quickly sped up the stairs.

She looked through the guest register for Eric's name. There it was; but it was crossed out. Perplexed, she half-turned, thinking of what to do next. *Perhaps he changed rooms?* Sure enough, his name appeared again on the next page: Room 2, second floor. Bobbie quickly sped up the stairs. She pushed on the door. It was not locked and, though very heavy, it flew open.

She immediately grabbed the edge of her jacket, covering her mouth and nose. The stench was horrible. Eric was lying on the bed in rumpled pajamas, covered in vomit and urine. His face was very gray.

Bobbie ran to him. "Eric, Eric," she said softly. She touched his arm; he was very warm. She moved close to his ear and spoke again, and his eyelids flickered. He was still alive.

A half-empty and soiled cup of water was on the bedside table. She took it to the bathroom to wash it out and refill it, and found that room in just as sorry a state. After quickly cleaning up the sink, Bobbie filled the glass and set the fresh water on the nightstand. Then she searched Eric's closet until she found a washcloth and towel. She stripped off his filthy clothing—no easy task—wet the cloth in the bathroom, then gently washed Eric's face and body. She had to rinse out the rag several times.

Bobbie went back to the closet and noticed his little food supply. After wrestling Eric (who was still barely conscious) into clean clothes, she grabbed a can of chicken noodle soup and a small kettle, then opened the can just enough to let the broth out. She returned to the bathroom sink for a third time and mixed cold and hot water into the kettle. She poured the chicken broth in and stirred it, then went back to Eric. She opened his mouth and tried to feed him a teaspoonful. His eyes remained closed but his body began to respond. Finally, after several tries, some soup at least had been swallowed. Eric gave a weak cough.

Next Bobbie turned Eric on his side and ripped off the sheets. Fortunately, the bed had a plastic mattress cover. She could not find clean sheets, so she had to use a blanket as a sheet and another as a bedspread. She tried giving him more soup, and he seemed to swallow a little.

She made up her mind to do her best to save him if it was her last act. Still, as time slipped by, Bobbie could see that Eric was going to have to be nursed for a few days. She could stay with him for one more, but then she'd have to talk to the building manager and have him notify whomever needed to know, probably his school at least, that Eric was sick and wouldn't be around for a while. Hopefully Junior knew Eric's friends or family and could make further arrangements to help take care of him.

Then what? Bobbie wondered. Was it time, once and for all, to leave the company? Despite her plans that morning, she'd now been missing long enough that someone would have noticed. What would happen if she returned? What would happen if she didn't? She touched her still-healing eye.

Eric was beginning to moan. His eyes fluttered open and closed, and color was coming back into his hands and face.

For many reasons Bobbie had never followed through on her dreams of leaving. But wasn't it different, now? With Eric, she had remembered that she was someone. To him, she was special. That simple fact had changed her. Perhaps she would go back to where she had grown up; a place she had never told anybody about. Sadly, whatever she decided, she could not tell Luce. That would be dangerous for both of them.

Bobbie got back to the task at hand. She gave Eric some water to drink. This seemed to be what he really needed, as his breathing became less labored. Perhaps the worst was over.

She nursed him through the night and the next morning, then at about 7:00 am she went to get the manager. Making sure the door would not lock behind her, she pulled it shut and ran down the stairs to the office.

She did not know the manager that well, only that his name was Junior and that he was gay. The word on the street was that he had a medical background and always seemed willing to help others. His door was ajar. She could smell coffee brewing and heard a radio in the background. *That's good*, she thought to herself. *Someone's awake.* Bobbie knocked loudly, and sure enough, Junior appeared in the doorway to his room behind the office. He was buttoning up his shirt.

"What is it?" he asked without looking up, gesturing for her to come in.

Bobbie took her shawl off, and immediately Junior recognized her.

"Bobbie! You know you're not supposed to be over here. The owner doesn't like ... but since you are ... what on earth can I do for you?"

She spoke quickly. "Eric has been deathly sick. I worry he might die if someone doesn't help him. He is hanging on by a thread." For the next minute or two, she explained the whole scenario.

"I'm in. Let me get my medical bag."

They quickly went to Eric's room. Junior seemed to know exactly what to do, so Bobbie became his helper. At noontime, they had Eric in reasonably good shape, so they paused.

"I need to go and tell the Romanos. Eric's really close with them," Junior explained. "I'll stop by and leave a note at the art school, too. Can you handle him while I'm gone?"

"Yes, of course," Bobbie said.

An hour later, Junior returned. By now Eric was definitely doing better, and Bobbie could see that her part was done. She was leaving Eric in good hands, and while she really wanted to stay with him, the handwriting was on the wall.

She touched Eric's face. She would always remember his quiet smile and the special look that he gave her. "He told me we were all God's children." Bobbie looked at the ceiling. "Well, God, he's all Yours now." Bobbie turned to Junior and whispered, "Thank you."

They looked back at Eric together, and he shook his head. "Thank *you*. You were his angel."

"Me, an angel?" Bobbie said. "That's a laugh." She paused at the door and reached out her hand, and Junior squeezed it. "I'm not sure that any of you will see me around anymore," she said. "Will you tell him goodbye for me?"

"Yes," Junior said. "Goodbye, Bobbie."

Bobbie quickly retraced her steps down the back stairs. She went through the back door, crossed the alley, and came to an intersection. She looked back, then turned and faced the street. People were moving back and forth and crossing the intersection. Everything behind her was familiar; everything in front of her was unknown. At least now, for the first time in many years, she felt truly loved.

The light changed. Bobbie wrapped her shawl around her head, tied it under her chin, then took a step.

CHAPTER 26

Surely He Will Save You

For the past four days, Monique had not slept. Something was wrong. Eric had always been communicative, especially with her mom. For instance, in the past, whenever he was not going to be able to be at the bus stop for some reason, he had always let Mom know.

Mom had not wanted her to go to Eric's hotel to find him because she was afraid of the people who hung out there. So instead, Monique had visited the art school several times. The administrative secretary was always very nice but kept telling her that he had not been in. "However," the secretary said one time, "if you are able to get in touch with him, please have him come into the office, get info for his summer classes, and clean out his locker." In her frantic search, Monique even tried to find Eric's friend Connie, but she was nowhere to be found.

Monique thought about how Eric had come under the scrutiny of the company. He was very smart, but he had a very naïve, almost childlike attitude toward life. He never spoke badly about anyone. He didn't seem to even perceive evil in others; probably because he wasn't looking for it. For some reason, he was slow to see how much danger he was in. She had worried about Uncle Dalio, but it had felt nothing like this. This was a level of concern which she had never experienced before. Her heart ached.

She remembered how Eric had reacted after Uncle Dalio's death; the gentle hugs he gave her and her mom and the way he would pray with them. The simplicity and honesty and straightforwardness of those prayers was foreign to her, but she had loved his earnest sincerity and emotional sensitivity. *He truly believed what he was saying*, she thought.

> "I don' t know where to begin," she said. "Help me. Help him. Please, God."

Eric never talked about church, but he was always saying how good God was. Monique was not used to reading the Bible, but she found Uncle Dalio's and started reading the Psalms. *Eric always mentioned Psalm 23 and Psalm 91*, she thought. Psalm 91:15 caught her attention: "He shall call upon me, and I will answer him: I will be with him in trouble; I will deliver him, and honour him."

She remembered many of the other times that Eric had prayed with them. And he prayed over food before he ate, and for safety. *Well, I need to pray*, she thought. *I need Eric's God to tell me where he could be. That's what Eric would do.*

Monique said to herself, "I don't know where to begin. Help me, help me. Help him. Please, God," she said. "Help me, help me, God. Help me. Help me." For some reason, she felt a whole lot better.

When the man entered her sandwich shop that Wednesday, Marisa somehow knew that he was there for a purpose other than to eat. She immediately guessed that it had something to do with Eric. He came to the counter and introduced himself as Junior. Marisa remembered conversations with Eric where that name had come up; he was the hotel manager.

The story of Eric's dilemma and Bobbie's discovery of him unfolded. "Until Eric is out of danger," Junior told Marisa, "he will need care. He is still too weak to move around." He continued, "Eric has mentioned you and your daughter a few times. I get the impression you are all close. Are you?"

Marisa nodded. She could sense where this was going.

Junior asked, "Do you think you can help him until he can again function on his own?"

"Yes, absolutely," Marisa answered. "I'll stop by as often as I can get away from the restaurant."

Junior seemed relieved. "Thank you," he said, then excused himself.

Monique returned from another one of her searches just as Junior was leaving. Marisa saw him nod politely to Monique as he walked out the door.

"Who was that?" Monique asked.

"That's the manager where Eric lives. He told me Eric has been sick. It sounds like he will be okay, but Junior asked me to help take care of him as he recovers."

"Where is Eric now?"

"In his room at the hotel," Marisa answered, and Monique sighed in relief. As Marisa explained the whole situation, her daughter grew agitated once more.

As soon as Marisa finished, Monique burst out, "Mom, I want to help, too."

"I'm not sure, Monique," Marisa said.

"Eric has done so much for me; for us. I have to help! Please!"

Marisa could see her daughter's earnestness. She thought long and hard while Monique waited for an answer.

Back in the day, there had been a completely different atmosphere on Third Street. It had bustled with activity, with shops of all kinds, including clockmakers and dry goods sellers. Nowadays the people who frequented the area where Eric lived were in such bad shape. Between that and all the drug trafficking, she felt uneasy at the thought of Monique spending time there without her.

Marisa had tried to protect Monique, and she still wanted to, but she could see Monique's desire to give back the help she'd received. And realistically, Marisa wouldn't be able to visit Eric as much as Monique could. Was there a way to make this work?

Then she thought, *What about Junior?*

Even though the hotel was at the end of the street, Junior was not someone Marisa had gotten to know. He almost never came to the store, and she and Monique didn't walk in that direction anymore. But she had heard the earnestness in his plea for help for Eric. Concern for a fellow human was unusual in this drug-infested environment. She remembered Eric mentioning that Junior had fixed Phillip's nose twice. Apparently, Junior used to be an army medic. She had had a good feeling talking to him, and she knew that Eric trusted him implicitly. She knew, somehow, that he was a kind and good man. Yes, Marisa felt confident that Monique would be okay with him, at least.

"Okay, Monique. But please check in with that manager, Junior, every time you're over there. And I'm going to call and ask if he'll walk you back home when it's dark out."

"Yes, Mom. Thank you, Mom!" Monique hugged her and ran out the door.

Marisa was not used to praying the way Eric prayed. It seemed so easy and informal for him to talk to God. She felt she couldn't connect without rosary beads, holding onto a cross, or burning candles. But she quietly said, "Please, God, help Monique and Eric. If you are their God, please, please help them."

She had found him! Monique started down the street, then slowed her pace and tried to walk normally. She didn't want to bring attention to herself. Finally, she reached the steps leading up to the double doors of Eric's hotel.

She noticed a musty old smell as she passed through the entrance. Across the lobby was the manager's desk area, but it was not in use. Monique looked around and noticed a makeshift sign that read *Hotel Office*. She walked quickly to the partially open door.

Junior was on the phone. As she pushed the door all the way open, he looked up with annoyance. Nevertheless he finished his call and motioned Monique to come over and sit down by his small table.

"How may I help you?" he asked kindly.

"I'm Monique," she answered. "My mother is Marisa, from the restaurant. She said you talked with her? I'm here to help with Eric. My mom knows; she said it was okay."

"Oh, well, hello, Monique! That was your mom on the phone," Junior said. "I'm grateful you're willing to help." His voice was kind, but Monique could tell he was skeptical. He continued, "Let me fill you in on what's happened and what he needs now."

Once more Monique listened patiently as Junior explained what had happened over the last two days. She paid closer attention when he began to describe the care Eric needed to receive. When he finished, she nodded. She understood exactly what needed to be done.

Monique waited as Junior went to his stove and got a warm kettle of soup that he had been heating up for Eric. The two of them then left the office and went upstairs to Eric's room. When they entered, Eric was lying on his back with his hands at his sides and a thin blanket covering him from his chest down. He looked fragile. Monique ran over to him and spoke softly.

He opened his eyes and gave her a tired smile. "Glad to see you," he murmured.

She smiled back and took his hand. His grip was not strong, but he was able to squeeze a little bit. *He must be very weak*, she thought.

Junior set the kettle on the nightstand. Monique filled a cup with soup. Lifting his head with her left hand, she was able to help him drink a little chicken broth. He drank very slowly, but it was going down. She smiled with joy to Junior, who looked pleased. "I think he'll be in good hands. I'll be downstairs if you need me."

Monique was so happy that she could help Eric. She was going to stay with him as long as it took to nurse him back to health.

CHAPTER 27

New Poses

It was good to be back. Connie had been away almost three weeks, and she had missed her apartment. The fact that Eric was in the city also made a difference. During her practicum Connie had had no contact with any teachers or students at the art school. Her studies had required her full attention. In her time away she had decided that she was going to pursue her master's degree in psychology. She would go to an out-of-state college that offered the program she wanted.

She recognized that this would disrupt the friendships that she had been developing over the past two years. She had really enjoyed the spiritual group at the school, and she truly would miss its influence in her life. She knew that she would not find such a loving and kind group anywhere else. To think that she hadn't had much interest when Johnny first invited her! Just to remain open-minded, she had decided to go. But she had found the group to be special. Each person was so kind and gentle that she immediately made up her mind to be part of it.

In fact, she was beginning to see every person she met in a new light. And her heart felt remorse for many of her past negative thoughts and actions. She was enjoying the transformative experience that Jesus and the Holy Spirit were making in her life.

She was embarking on a new life. She was beginning to be born again. "Thank you, Jesus," she said to herself.

Connie thought again of Eric. They had become quite close before she left. She felt drawn to him on several levels, which was very different from her previous relationships. It was another irony, since when she first met Eric, he had seemed extremely focused and intense.

Connie noticed that Eric was almost never at the center of a conversation, even during critique sessions. He always remained a quiet observer, willing to take criticism. If he disagreed with a point of view, he did it respectfully. At first, she thought he didn't have any backbone. She had written him off as just another guy who hadn't grown up yet. *How could he possibly fit in her world?* she had wondered.

But she had misjudged him. After months of modeling, she began to see the respect the students and teachers showed him. He was very talented, but there was something else. At first she couldn't put her finger on it, but eventually she understood: he showed humility, kindness, decency, and respect toward others. Putting others first set him apart.

She found him to be a concerned conversationalist. Soon she wanted more of his company, and her instincts had told her to take it easy. It was as if he was too easy to know. There was no game-playing; no hidden agenda in his words or actions. Eric seemed so young and innocent. He took some getting used to; and he needed more time … a lot more.

On Friday as she entered the art school, her thoughts were quickly pulled back to the reality of her modeling career. She checked into the office and was greeted by the front desk clerk. She got her assignment for the week's modeling sessions, then walked to the drawing studio to look at the art pinned to the wall. Most of the drawings, in her estimation, were very good. She continued walking the halls. Connie enjoyed art; at one time she had considered painting as a career.

It was late when she returned to her apartment. As she passed Third Street, memories of Eric once more flooded her mind. She had hated to leave him, and while away he had been a sweet fragrance to her, but now she had conflicting thoughts. Why?

Being the middle of January, it was very cold. Connie pulled her down coat tighter to her. She wiped thoughts of Eric from her mind as she opened the door to the apartment. She turned up the heat and threw herself onto the couch without removing any clothing. There she fell fast asleep.

At 4:00 in the morning Connie awoke to more thoughts of Eric and could not get back to bed. She couldn't expect him to leave art school to follow her in her career. He wouldn't want her to give up her own goals to follow him, either. *Do I really love him?* she thought. *Could I love a person who sometimes doesn't seem to know enough to come in out of the rain?*

She remained deep in these thoughts while she took her shower and ate a breakfast of coffee and buttered toast. She finally looked at the time, and realized she had to get to work. She wasn't going to be late, but it would be close. She walked fast and reached the school in good time. She stepped into the models' dressing room and quickly changed into her gown.

Now her mind was in a more familiar mode. She was the actor. After a few words from the drawing instructor, she removed her gown and stood at the center of the room for thirty drawing students. During her fifteen-minute break, she put her gown back on and then walked around the room, looking at the drawings. She noticed that Eric was not there, but she didn't think too much about it. Johnny would know where he was.

They talked during a break between poses. Johnny told her that Eric had been very sick. "The building manager where Eric lives won't let anyone see him. He wouldn't even let me go up."

Connie had interacted with Junior on some of her prior visits to Eric's place. She decided she would talk to him for herself and see what information he could provide.

CHAPTER 28

Warrior Medics

Junior had learned in the war that under fire, your mind gets clear and the survival of each member of your team becomes paramount. Your senses become acutely aware of everything, big and small.

He noticed an intensity in Monique's attitude, an interest and maturity of focus that was very unusual for someone her age. She was all there: no nonsense, no heroics, no hysterics. Her whole body was in accord with itself. Her movements were natural but controlled. He marveled at Monique. This was her moment to be a warrior for someone else; for her friend. Even on that first day when he left her with Eric and made his way back downstairs to the office, he knew that Eric was being well cared for.

Junior wasn't religious, but after two tours in Vietnam and seeing so much evil, he had begun to believe in God. The bottom line was that he saw the difference between love and hate. The devastation created by war had pushed him in the other direction. He could not look at the enemy as inhuman. He could never kill just to kill. That's why he had chosen to be a medic. He realized that Monique was driven by a similar caring spirit; a love that was the essence of her being and upbringing. He had not noticed it before, but she had teamed up with God, even if she didn't realize it.

Then there was Eric. Everyone seemed to be drawn to this kid. Since he had arrived, Junior had worried that he would get disillusioned. He was so completely out of place. There was a constant ebb and flow of art students in the hotel who were overcome by city life. Some were from "down on the farm," you might say, and they would leave for home after just a few weeks. Some became homesick and left after a few months. Other students took the opportunity to buy drugs off the street. They became part of the society that used drugs on social occasions, at parties, and so on.

Over time Junior noticed that Eric did not get involved with any of this. He seemed to have a good name and a very good-natured attitude toward all comers. He didn't reject anyone. One evening he had seen Eric in front of the hotel on the concrete with the winos, passing the cheap wine down the line. *Why would he do that?* Junior still wondered. Sitting in the stench of cheap wine and urine with a group of older men who were so drunk they couldn't stand up, let alone walk, unless it was to fight—there wasn't an evening that went by without one—it was beyond Junior's comprehension. Those two brothers who lived on the third floor and were always beating each other up were part of that group of winos. They were big, strong guys, and Eric could be badly hurt (Mr. Jones had Junior clean their room once a week because it was always such a huge mess; a war zone, as it were). Yet Eric somehow took all of this in with a good-natured shrug of the shoulders and a smile.

Junior had heard an expression: "Fools go where angels fear to tread." However, Eric was no fool. How could he sum up Eric? So far, he hadn't been able to.

It was late Friday afternoon, and Monique had done all she could for Eric that day. She pulled the single chair up by the bed. She intended to watch him, but she was so worn out that she fell asleep sitting upright.

CHAPTER 29

A Stilled Life

At that very moment, across from Romano's, something unusual was going on. The police showed up in several squad cars. They parked diagonally, blocking the street so that no cars could pass. Marisa looked out and saw that the police had blocked off the end of the street in both directions as well. An ambulance was allowed to enter; it parked in front of the building that was home to Luce and Bobbie.

Marisa had been watching for Monique's return. She was later than usual, and Marisa was just about ready to go to the hotel to look for her when she received a call from Junior. He told her that he'd found Monique sleeping, and once they finished settling Eric, he would walk her back over to the restaurant.

Marisa went back to the window and watched the proceedings across the street. The back of the ambulance was open, and someone on a stretcher was being put in. The figure under the blanket was motionless. Fear began to creep into the back of Marisa's brain. *Who*

could that be, she wondered? The doors to the ambulance were abruptly closed, then it pulled around the police cars and drove slowly away. No sirens or lights; just a quiet ambulance heading toward the center of town.

As she continued to watch, the police brought out a large man in handcuffs. He had a jacket over his head, so Marisa could not tell who he was, but he looked vaguely familiar. The police pushed his head down and shoved him through the open door of a squad car. He didn't seem to resist. An officer got in beside him and closed the door. The squad car backed away from the curb and drove up the street, lights flashing but no siren.

Something major was happening, but she could only guess what it was. As she tried to process it all, the summer school crowd started to show up for supper. Marisa began taking orders.

A Stilled Life

CHAPTER 30

Among the Living

It was already Saturday afternoon; Monique had slept for some time. She dressed quickly, ate, and wrote a note for her mom. She tried not to look at the police barricades as she hurried over to Eric's apartment.

He was awake. She found the laundry closet in the hall and got two guest pillows, then she helped prop him up in a semi-seated position with the pillows supporting his back against the headboard. "I'll make you some food," she said.

Monique took the kettle into the bathroom and turned on the light. There was a large mirror, and she stood there looking at herself. She could see the bathroom window behind her. Just like the first time she'd visited to care for Eric, it was still broken and covered with plastic.

Monique had never been a superficial person. She had always gone to Mass with her mom. She had always gone to confession. She had read the Catechism and developed a certain amount of fear about Heaven and hell and purgatory. But what only a few weeks ago seemed to be big priorities now seemed of no importance.

After mixing some soup, she stood next to Eric and spoon-fed him more chicken broth. Eric was very pale, his usual smile was a bit weak, and he had dark circles under his eyes; but today he was able to speak. He was making progress.

At about 7:00 in the evening, Junior visited. He had been so busy with hotel guests all afternoon that he had not been by yet that day.

"How are you doing?" Junior asked Eric.

"I don't feel so good," he answered, "but Monique has been here all day and has really helped me. She's been great."

Junior nodded. "She sure has."

Monique said to Junior, "My mom is going to start worrying if I stay much longer. I told her I would be home before dark."

> Monique reached out and squeezed Eric's hand. Eric looked down at her hand and held it for a moment.

Eric spoke. "You can go. I can take care of myself from here. My strength is coming back. I'm pretty sure I'll feel a lot better after a good night's rest. I may even go in to school in the next couple of days."

Junior looked at his watch. "I'll stop by later, Eric. I told Marisa that I would walk Monique home."

Monique reached out and squeezed Eric's hand. Eric looked down at her hand and held it for a moment.

"Thank you so much," he said, and let go.

She got up from the chair and gave a sweet smile. "See you tomorrow."

She and Junior left the room, closing the door behind them.

Eric's head wasn't throbbing anymore, and he didn't ache all over. He sat on the edge of his bed. After a while, he stood up. His strength was coming back quickly, but he could tell he was still weak. He knew he had been very sick, but he still didn't comprehend what had taken place. Was it food poisoning, or something more nefarious? He only knew that he had to get to school soon to clean his locker out. The art school was quite strict about that.

Eric walked slowly to the bathroom and then back to the bed. He sat down and then laid back on the pillows once again. It sure felt good to be back among the living. Eric fell sound asleep.

CHAPTER 31

A High Price

On Sunday afternoon Connie walked down Third Street toward Eric's building. She was used to seeing a bustling crowd of students and sailors walking to and fro, but there were hardly any people out and about, even though it was only 4:00.

When she got close to Romano's, Connie saw the police barricades closing off the sidewalk for about fifty feet. No cars were parked there, and no one could go in or out. It looked completely deserted. Romano's was open, but there were few guests.

Connie was still wondering what had happened when she reached the hotel. She opened the front door and was surprised to see the lobby full of activity. She found Junior in his office. He seemed to immediately recognize her. He motioned for her to come in and offered her a chair. Connie was caught off guard by Junior's demeanor. He acted much older than he was. He had a very businesslike exterior, and he also exhibited great tact.

She said, "I hear Eric is in quarantine. How is he?"

Junior smiled. "He's doing quite well now, thank you. He was very sick for several days and basically hasn't left his room. I haven't been allowing any of his friends to see him because he was too weak even to talk. He's asleep right now, but just yesterday he said he hopes to stop by the school soon."

In light of this, Connie wasn't going to argue about seeing Eric. She was about to leave when she remembered:

"Junior," she said, "Do you know why the police barricades are on Third Street?"

"Yeah, I do," he said. "Two days ago a prostitute was beaten to death in the upstairs apartment by her managing pimp, who also was a dealer. He was known in our community as someone to avoid. A plainclothes policeman was nearby and saw what happened. He called the police, they surrounded the place, and the perpetrator gave up without a fight."

Connie was horrified. She thought of things that she had heard about the neighborhood. She also remembered things that Eric had said; people and experiences he had spoken about. Was the woman who'd been killed the one Eric always prayed for?

"Do you want to hear more?" Junior asked.

Connie nodded.

"She was one of the two older streetwalkers who lived and worked out of the second-floor apartment across from Romano's restaurant." Junior paused, distracted. "Bobbie was over here not quite a week ago. She's the one who found Eric. Saved him, as a matter of fact.

"I haven't seen her at all since that night. My guess—my hope—is that the company hasn't seen her, either. I think they wanted to track her down, and they sent someone to question Luce about it. But she must have been unable or unwilling to give them the information they wanted.

"The rest is history. No one heard any screams, but when the plainclothes cop went into the room, Luce was already dead. It doesn't appear that her killer realized that she was dead because he was still in the building."

Connie frowned. "Does Eric know about this?" she asked.

Junior answered, "No, he does not! And I am not about to tell him until I am sure he has recovered."

"I won't say anything to him, either, then. Junior, I must go. Maybe we can talk more later." Junior nodded. "Goodbye, and thank you," Connie said. She walked through the lobby and out the front door. It was now evening. For some reason, she felt a whole lot better.

CHAPTER 32

The Old Has Gone

By Tuesday Eric was fully on his feet. That day, he and Junior talked for over an hour about everything that had taken place while he was ill. He was still thinking about all of it as he walked down Third Street on his way to school. The police barriers were still up as he passed by. He stopped in front of Romano's and looked up to where Bobbie had sat in her window. It seemed depressing and desolate.

He could still hear her voice calling out. When Junior had told him what she had done, Eric had become very concerned for Bobbie. Junior had given what assurance he could, but it remained unclear to either of them just where she had gone. Eric could only hope that she was in a much better place.

As for Luce, Eric had not had a relationship with her or anyone else on that side of the street, but he felt sorry for all involved. And now the company apparently had moved out. Luce's death had been a catalyst for law enforcement to move in more aggressively to clean up the town of prostitution and drugs. The company had been given an ultimatum to clear out or be prosecuted on all fronts, including income tax evasion.

Deep in thought, he continued to school. Everything was different. Now that he was well enough (and safe enough?) to continue, he felt confident about further developing his skills by taking summer classes. He also decided to take the job the museum director had offered him for the summer.

He crossed High Street, went up the steps, and entered the art school. The office was open. He picked up the key to his locker and started down the hall. As he walked by the drawing studio, he realized that he would soon see Connie for the first time since she had left for her practicum.

Eric opened his locker. He took out his portable easel and his two tackle boxes. One had carving tools in it, the other had drawing tools. He looked for any art and painting supplies that might have fallen to the bottom of the locker. Back in the office, he leaned his boxes and easel against the wall and returned the key. Then he sat down and waited for class to get out.

The office secretary wanted to know how he was doing, so he told her some of his story. She was very kind.

"It's good to have you back," she said. "Several students have been asking about you."

Johnny and several other art students came by on their way out of class. Eric did not see Connie.

"Hey there, you!" said Johnny. "We have all missed you. Want to join us for supper? We're all getting together at my place in about an hour, one final time, to say farewell to some of our fellow artists who are leaving. We would love to have you there. I have something special to announce to our group, so I really need you to come if you can."

Eric was quite curious. Everyone seemed excited.

"Okay, Johnny, I will be there. But I can't stay too long as I'm still a bit under the weather."

"Great," said Johnny.

The others walked away together down the street, while Eric carried his art stuff back to the hotel.

His mind reverted to Bobbie and Luce. Romano's was even closed, now, as he passed by. Why? He couldn't imagine. He reached his room,

put his stuff away, and washed his face in the bathroom sink. It really was good to be back among the living, but he felt a little worse for wear. Eric sat in his room and leaned his head back on the chair, trying to rest.

He realized that he had not seen Monique or Mrs. Romano today. Then he thought, *I need to pray for all my friends and my relationships.* Eric knelt on the rug and prayed for each of them. When he got up from his knees, he felt somewhat rejuvenated.

He put on a clean shirt and pants and combed his hair. Downstairs, Junior's door was open, but he was not at his desk. Eric left the hotel and walked the eight blocks to Johnny's place.

CHAPTER 33

I Prepare a Place for You

Johnny lived on the second floor of an old Victorian home in a residential district of the city. He had been able to get it at a quite reasonable rent because he took care of the maintenance of the home and mowed the lawn in the summer. The couple who owned it were quite old. They really liked Johnny and helped him pay for his school. He basically had the second floor to himself, which was good since he liked to have a lot of people around.

Eric followed the sidewalk around the side to where steps led up to the second-floor landing. There was an entryway enclosure large enough for several people, and he could hear the sound of a large crowd within. *Leave it to Johnny.* Eric had to knock loudly a couple of times before the door was flung open.

Johnny smiled and said loudly, "Welcome, Eric. Follow me." He ushered Eric into a large parlor with comfortable seats all around, including a couple of easy chairs and a sofa. "Before I make my important announcement, have a bite to eat."

A long counter against the wall was loaded with food. Eric got a small plate and helped himself. He found a place to sit out of the way and started looking around the room at the guests. Many of them he did not know, but there were some older students that he had been in classes with from the beginning. He finished his plate of food and got up to get some fruit for dessert.

As he reloaded his plate, he heard a voice say, "Eric! Eric, it's so good to see you up and around." It was Connie. "I went by your hotel to see you the other day, but Junior said you were asleep and not to disturb you. I was waiting to see you when you came back to school. You look great, Eric," she said.

"I'm glad to see you as well," Eric said. "I was wondering where you were. Thanks for coming by. I was pretty sick, I guess. It's taken a while for me to get back on my feet." Eric paused. "Maybe we can find time to talk sometime tonight."

"Sounds good." Connie touched his arm. Then she turned, pulled up a chair, and started conversing with Pastor Ken of the Adventist church.

Well, this is a surprise, Eric thought. Both the pastor and his wife were there. For the first time that evening, Eric started to feel uneasy. *Okay*, he thought to himself, *what is going on?*

Just then Johnny stood in the opening between the two rooms and held up his hand for everyone to be quiet. "As you know, I have something to tell you tonight, so listen up.

"I have been at the art school for four years now. I feel confident in my artistic talent and in the fact that God has helped me develop beyond what I hoped for. But the greatest gift has been my developing friendships with all of you. Not just friends, but brothers and sisters in Christ.

"I asked Pastor Ken and his wife to join us because he has been so instrumental in our learning and understanding of Scripture. Through his ministry at the art school and his Wednesday night meetings, all of us here tonight have been brought face-to-face with Jesus Christ. I believe that Pastor Ken has baptized most of us in this room. So thank you, Pastor Ken."

Eric continued to feel quite uneasy as Johnny spoke. Johnny continued:

"We would also like to thank each of our other friends who may not have been verbal, but who have lived as Christ would have lived in front of us. They too have been strong witnesses for Jesus. Most of you, by this time, know who they are, but I know that they prefer to be nameless so I'm not going to mention them. You know who you are. We thank you."

> Four years ago, I was an atheist. Now, I believe in a risen Savior and life eternal.

At this, everyone clapped.

Johnny reached the end of his discourse: "Jesus created us to begin with. Then He came to this earth and He died for us, taking all our sins upon Himself so that we could have eternal life. His death on the cross secured for us life. Four years ago, I was an atheist. Now, I believe in a risen Savior and life eternal."

Eric started to relax. Ever since the incident with Phillip and the drug dealer when his own thinking and life had changed completely, he had hoped that each of his friends would also see and feel the love of Jesus.

There was a commotion at the door. The crowd of guests became silent as Johnny welcomed more people. As he turned from the door with a big smile, two individuals followed him into the room and Eric almost fell from his chair.

Monique and Mrs. Romano stood quietly in the center of the room as Johnny made introductions. Monique seemed perfectly at ease. Many of the students also welcomed Mrs. Romano. Some obviously knew her from the sandwich shop.

Can you beat that? Eric thought as he watched quietly from the sideline. He recognized how far out of the loop he was. He kept saying to himself, "Thank you, Jesus."

CHAPTER 34

The Greatest Artist

For the past week and a half, while Eric had been sick, Monique had been visiting church at Johnny's and Connie's invitation. She and Connie had actually become acquainted some time before in the sandwich shop. They had once talked over a meal about a modeling career and what that entailed.

Earlier in the week of the party, Monique had asked Johnny if Eric would be there. Johnny had assured her that he would do his best to get Eric to come, but they both knew very well that Eric was very quiet and shy. She thought to herself, *I'm going anyway, even if he doesn't come.* She had been drawn into this group of friends, with or without Eric.

Johnny had finished his introductions. Now the pastor welcomed her and her mom. Monique watched her mom discover what she already knew, which was why everyone liked him so much. He had an energy that was catching and a quick, genuine smile. She could tell her mom immediately liked him. This was Monique's first time really talking with the pastor's wife; she was much more reserved, but she had a kind face, and her smile was genuine as well.

Her eyes finally rested on Eric, sitting out of the way in the shadows. She walked around several small groups of people who were standing and talking quietly and came to where he was.

Eric gave her a sheepish smile. "Boy, you sure surprised me!" he said. "Both you and your mom."

She smiled back. "Well, if you were around more often, these things would not be such a surprise."

Eric realized now why he had been put in this position. He had needed to be broken down by the Spirit of God. His pride, selfishness, and arrogance had to be taken away. He could now see that God, through the Holy Spirit, had made him useful even though he was still somewhat skeptical.

Why am I still skeptical? he wondered. Mrs. Romano and Monique had made a choice to follow Jesus and leave a system he felt was corrupt. Until tonight, he had had no idea. To Eric, this was very strange. Very strange, indeed. They were two of the finest people he had ever met.

Eric remembered Romans 6:23: "For the wages of sin is death, but the gift of God is eternal life through Jesus Christ our Lord." *One still must have free choice to follow Jesus or follow the evil, selfish plans of men,* he thought. *We choose to follow Jesus because we see in Him His loving character, His unselfishness, how He is always willing to serve others first before Himself.*

This does not mean, Eric thought, *that we are trodden down and stepped on, but that we are more interested in lifting others toward the God who created us. By doing so, we become the material that Heaven is made of. Focusing on Christ's life and accepting His grace changes our lives. Our sins are forgiven, and we are able to live under His banner.*

Monique was conversing with someone else while Eric was lost in these thoughts. She now turned to him again with a gentle smile and asked, "What do you think of all these people, some of whom you don't even know, who have chosen to follow Jesus because of a few art students like you? You have given us a glimpse of Jesus by example."

"I really had no idea all this was going on," said Eric. "I can't take any of the credit. I recognize where all good things really come from." Anyway, Eric knew that Johnny had been the real instrument that God had used to pull all this together.

"I have avoided church because of all the restrictions that were placed on me as a kid," Eric said. "I really didn't want any part of it. But over the last three years, and the experiences that these years brought me, my life has changed for the better. I am convinced now that Jesus is my guide, and that each person I meet is one of His children who needs to be lifted up and respected."

"What has drawn me to you," Monique said in a very quiet tone, sincere and respectful, "and it's probably the case for many others in this room, is the unqualified love that you have shown us. What I mean is that I feel at peace when I am around you. I believe this is God's peace.

"I just want to thank you for being part of my life and putting up with all our family troubles. My mom and I want to be baptized into your church. I know you don't like church, but maybe you could go with us sometime." She smiled and went to join her mother.

Eric sat there dumbfounded. He wasn't sure he was prepared for all of this. He thought to himself, *Maybe Monique is right. Church may not be so bad after all.* He felt good. Maybe at long last, God was able to use him despite a messed-up life.

Pastor Ken stood up. He started to speak about the fruits of the Spirit in 1 Corinthians 13; then how Jesus had shown, from the time He was a child until He went to His death on the cross, true love for each and every person He ran across. Pastor Ken then spoke about the peace and joy that comes with a life reflecting Jesus. He spoke quietly and reflectively. All were listening intently.

Someone sat down beside Eric and spoke to him in a low voice. "He is really a great pastor, isn't he?" Connie was smiling at him. "He is a true believer and a student of the Bible."

She went on, "Since I have been back, you and I have not been able to get together, what with everything that has gone on. I wanted to let you know how much I have appreciated getting to know you, and the wonderful influence you have had on my life. I will never forget you, Eric."

"Thank you, Connie, for the kind words. You have taught me a lot about many things; mostly through your kind and caring attitude, especially in a very selfish world." Eric went on, "Also, you taught me to have a profound respect for the nude model. Drawing well is a discipline, and respect for the hard work of an accomplished model is very important for an artist. There must be a proper distance, physically and mentally."

She put her hand on his arm. "I will be leaving to go to college out of state in a few days. I won't see you again for some time." She looked into his eyes as if searching for something.

Eric said, "Connie, you and I drew very close this school year. It was a special time for both of us, I think. I'm going to miss you, but it is always good to follow our dreams. We are going our separate ways for some very good reasons. But maybe we could stay in touch."

Connie looked at the diminishing crowd, and a smile crossed her face. With tears in her eyes, she said, "I'm really going to miss you, too. And yes, let's keep in touch." She got up, put her arms around Eric, and hugged him. "Goodbye," she said.

Eric overheard Johnny tell the pastor that he was going to drive Connie home, and then he would come back so they could talk about the upcoming church service. Connie walked to the door, then looked back and smiled once more. Eric smiled back.

Not long after, Eric said his goodbyes and stepped through the door into the cold night. He went down the steps and started toward his hotel. After only a few steps, someone called his name. He turned. It was Monique and her mom.

"We thought you would like company walking home." Monique said. "Come on, let's walk fast. It's cold out here." She grabbed his hand, and they picked up the pace.

As they walked back to Romano's, Eric saw how excited they were to be experiencing their newfound faith; the saving grace of Christ. It almost seemed that they had been infused with some special energy. Eric thought, *I wish I had that kind of excitement about spiritual stuff.*

It was difficult for him to accept the fact that the Holy Spirit had used him as a conduit in all these people's lives. Was it okay to be a little bit proud of his friends' decisions?

No: he couldn't take credit for any of their decisions for Christ. Pride had no place.

CHAPTER 35

Illuminating Grace

Breakfast was almost over at Romano's, and the local crowd had diminished. Eric found an empty table toward the back and sat down. He hadn't slept much the night before, as his mind had been occupied with so many different thoughts.

Mrs. Romano had asked that he stop by on his way to work in the morning. She had said she wanted to talk to him about things important to her, including the church. He wasn't sure what he could offer, but he had agreed. He only knew that he couldn't even come close to the Romanos in compassion and kindness. And he certainly felt like he didn't have any patience compared to what they exhibited. He was dumbfounded that they esteemed him at all.

He certainly wasn't ready for any theological discussions or questions, if that was what Mrs. Romano wanted to talk about. He was no Pastor Ken. Pastor Ken had such energy for Christ, and he energized and motivated others naturally. It was just the way he was. Thinking about Pastor Ken was a little depressing … yet Eric was drawn to him. *Go figure*, he thought. *Anyway, what does all this mean?*

Eric felt he was a religious reject. His attitude was still that church symbolized restrictions and rules that seemed to be so out of step with the Jesus that he had come to know. To him, the love of Jesus was very simple.

What were the rules that Jesus functioned under? Eric thought to himself. *He gave up His personal interests for the overall well-being of His friends and neighbors.* And Eric recognized that Jesus did a lot of praying to His Father in heaven while here on Earth. *Goodness, kindness, and peace belong to Jesus.* How could *he*, Eric, have reflected any of that? He did not know.

What did *happen at the cross?* he thought. *Was it the end of death?* He decided that if you took all the superficial rules away from the Adventists and got down to the bottom line, they truly believed that Jesus was coming back to save those who had proved to love God and their fellow man humbly and meekly.

They have no arrogance, no self-interest, and no self-righteousness. They are just doing their best to get to know Jesus and share the life they have with Him. Eric wasn't sure, but he felt he had hope in this love.

Eric stared toward the front window, through which he could still see part of the police barricade across the street. He was still unsure of what had happened. But Bobbie was gone, and Luce was dead; that he did know. His mind went back two and a half years as he thought about them. He hadn't really known either of them very well, but Bobbie had brought out something in him; something unique and special.

How could he have ever related to a person like her? Why hadn't he taken one street over to go to school? She was so much of a user and such a mess. She had been so abused. She swore at him every time he went by with such anger and loudness. Yet he had seen her change from someone who showed her anger to someone who seemed to be more at peace. He was unsure of many things about her, but the change in her attitude toward him was very real. Strangely enough, he missed her a great deal. There was an empty place in his heart. He tried to put her out of his mind.

Eric was jarred back to reality by the smell of scrambled eggs and toast. Mrs. Romano was standing by his table with his breakfast on a tray. She was looking at him with that gentle smile of hers, waiting for him to come back to Earth.

Eric said, "I'm sorry. I'm just not myself this morning."

She leaned over the table and looked at Eric intently. "You were very sick. It takes a while to get back your energy and your positivity. You need time to rest.

"Now, don't worry: I didn't ask you to come here to grill you about religion or anything else. I don't have a need to know about your distant past. I just like you being part of us. As Monique has said on numerous occasions, when you're around, she feels a peace come over her. Monique and I are your friends. And, yes, we consider you to be family. You are alone, but we want you to know that you have us to count on."

Eric stopped her. "Please, I don't know what to say. My mom must have done something right by how she brought me up. But I'm not that good a person. I'm not even sure how to live. I lack an understanding of spiritual things, and I certainly don't have a good understanding of the Bible."

No new customers had come into the shop, so Mrs. Romano sat down opposite Eric and continued.

"Monique and I know you are not perfect. We see someone who, without trying, is kind and humble. You are not judgmental. Your treatment of Luce and Bobbie was nothing short of remarkable. Since you have been in our neighborhood, you have had a very positive effect on all of us. Monique and I have even become closer as a family because of your presence in our lives.

"I have thought a lot about you, and I asked you to come here this morning because I wanted to tell you. I want to thank you for helping us through a very difficult time and teaching us how to pray directly to Jesus."

After she finished speaking, the two of them sat there quietly. Eric just thought, not saying a word.

Monique came through the front door just then and walked over to the table, smiling. She pulled up a chair and sat down. "Good morning, Eric."

Eric smiled at her and said to them both, "You know, the two of you have convinced me of my need for a church family. I would like to be part of *your* family."

CHAPTER 36

On Solid Ground

The next day, after his shift at the museum, Mrs. Romano, Monique, and Eric prepared a lunch and took a bus to the Eastern Promenade, a park overlooking the bay in front of the city. It was a cold, late-spring day. For a moment they stood at the railing, looking down the cliff at the beautiful blue of the ocean and the breakwater farther out to sea. Several sailboats heeled in the wind. They seemed to move slowly over the water, tacking back and forth. Mrs. Romano and Monique went and sat down on a park bench in a small grove that was protected from the cold wind by high bushes. Eric stayed at the railing for a moment longer.

Three and a half years ago, he had been out there, sailing beyond the breakwater. He had prayed to God that day to rescue him from a very cold death. He looked over to where Monique and her mom were feeding the ever-present pigeons. He walked toward them with a smile on his face. Yes, he knew that God had saved him that day long ago and given him a purpose for his life. His friends were living proof.

One of his favorite Bible verses, John 3:16, came to mind: "For God so loved the world, that he gave his only begotten Son, that whosoever believeth in him should not perish, but have everlasting life." Eric couldn't help but praise God. This was not the end. It was the beginning of his life in Jesus.

On Solid Ground

EPILOGUE

At Home

Eric's mother had always felt like she didn't know enough to raise a child. She had only a fourth-grade education; she felt handicapped. But she was brought up a Christian, and she read everything she could find about history. She also started reading the Bible when she was very young. Almost all of her education was based on the Bible and books by church pioneers.

Her goal was to teach the Bible's principles, so she taught cradle roll in Sabbath School for thirty years. As a mother, it was an outlet for her own needs. Meanwhile she spent many years praying for her prodigal son. Her peace was in Jesus, and eventually her prayers were answered.

Eric's choices in life were directly influenced by his mother and by the dramatic contrast between good and evil which he witnessed. After he finished school, he stayed in the city for a while and worked in the art museum.

Mrs. Romano and Monique kept up their friendship with him, and he became a permanent guest at their home. Monique was Eric's best friend. Each week she asked him to accompany them to "the Sabbath church." Eventually he started going (although his interest remained a little hesitant). Many years later, Monique and Eric married.

Together they continued to have a positive spiritual influence on those around them, and Eric's mother died knowing that her prodigal son believed in Jesus as his personal Friend and Savior.

Bibliography

White, Ellen. *Education*. Mountain View, CA: Pacific Press Publishing Association, 1903.

White, Ellen. *Mind, Character, and Personality, Volume 1*. Nashville, TN: Southern Publishing Association, 1977.

We invite you to view the complete
selection of titles we publish at:
www.TEACHServices.com

We encourage you to write us
with your thoughts about this,
or any other book we publish at:
info@TEACHServices.com

TEACH Services' titles may be purchased in
bulk quantities for educational, fund-raising,
business, or promotional use.
bulksales@TEACHServices.com

Finally, if you are interested in seeing
your own book in print, please contact us at:
publishing@TEACHServices.com
We are happy to review your manuscript at no charge.

www.ingramcontent.com/pod-product-compliance
Lightning Source LLC
Chambersburg PA
CBHW070551160426
43199CB00014B/2465